PEACE OF MIND
for MONEY
MATTER$

Teri Rogowski, CFP®, CSA

Dedication

I dedicate this book to my mom in heaven, who taught me
to be truthful, kind and gentle. She took great pride in all
of my accomplishments, big and small.
May she Rest In Peace

To my sister, Joann Steffens, who has been my greatest advocate
and introduced me to the world of finance and investments

To my children, who gave me strength to keep moving
forward no matter what happens,
Gloria, Julie, Donny & Mike

Acknowledgements

There are far too many people to mention who played a part in this book coming to life. A few I would like to mention and thank include:

- My brother, Bob and sister-in-law, Selene Schmittling. The first to encourage and support me in a decision to launch my own business.
- My daughter-in law, Nina Perez, who wrote and self-published years before I had the courage; she has been a great inspiration.
- My daughter-in-law, Valerie Bauschka, who was the first to read my first couple of paragraphs and has been cheering me on ever since.
- My granddaughter, Katie Carr, for the illustrations.
- My publishing and book marketing consultant, Diana M. Needham, who told me, "There are people out there waiting for your book." She kept me motivated and on track.
- My editor, Nanette Levin, who encouraged me to expand my writing into my own experiences and knowledge.
- Branding expert and author, Annie Franceschi, for her creativity and encouragement.
- My beta readers, Karen O'Malley, Nora Rhode and Anne Pippin. Your encouragement and suggestions early on were invaluable.

Thank you to all of my relatives, friends, colleagues and clients. I could not have done this without you.

Table of Contents

A Special Bonus Gift from Teri

Now that you have your copy of **Peace of Mind for Money Matter$**, you are on your way to moving from confused and overwhelmed to realizing clarity, control and confidence over your own finances!

As an owner of my book, I am offering a special bonus I created to add to your toolkit –**Financial Organizing Essentials**. This is a variety of tools that will help you and your loved ones gain control over financial matters that are certain to arise. The checklists, worksheets and resource links will streamline financial tasks that are often overwhelming and provide families with peace of mind.

While the **Financial Organizer Essentials** is offered for sale, as a special bonus you can claim it for free here:
http://www.day2daypersonalfinancial.com/bonus

The sooner you learn the financial basics covered in this book, the better your chances of having peace of mind over your own money matters.

I'm in your corner. Let me know if I can help further.

Here's to Clarity, Control and Confidence over your financial life.

Best,

Teri

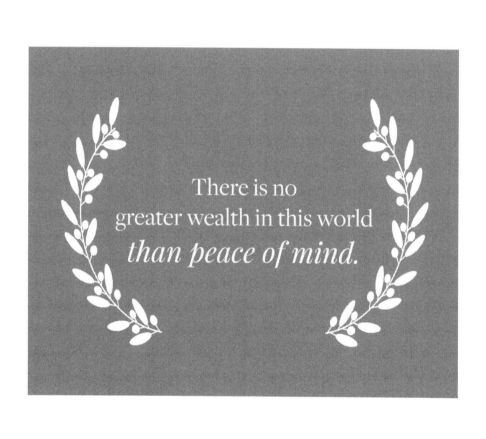

There is no
greater wealth in this world
than peace of mind.

Introduction

I have spent several decades guiding individuals and families to plan for their financial future. People now see me as a highly knowledge-able personal financial caretaker. This was not always the case. There was a time in my life when I was consumed with terror over simple financial tasks and decisions. I want to begin by sharing a story about my earlier life.

Opening the mail that day in May should have brought a sense of relief. Receiving a check should do that, right? It was a check from an insurance company. I did not feel at all relieved. In fact, there was a new sense of dread. Will this pain ever subside? I thought I would be sick as that feeling once again rose up from the depths of my stomach. I tell myself, "You cannot get sick, cry, or get angry. You must not show any emotion that could upset the children."

It had only been two months since that day that forever changed my life. The events kept running through my mind. I was called into my boss's office. He had a visitor, my husband's boss, which seemed so odd. They proceeded to tell me that there had been an accident. My husband, Don, had died at the scene. Everything moved in slow motion. I had no idea what to do! This made no sense. I had just seen him a few hours ago.

As I look back to this incident 33 years ago, it is like those few moments in time occurred just yesterday. The numbness is deeply imprinted into my memory. That day remains ingrained as the most difficult day of my life. The task of telling my children that their dad had died was by far the most heart-wrenching thing I have ever had to do. It was my daughter's 16th birthday and my youngest son would be 7 in three days. Those two days, which should be times of celebrations, were forever changed.

Little did I know that the events of that day and the months that followed would provide me with invaluable lessons and experiences. I would develop a passion to work with people who felt alone and lost in financial matters. I would go on many years later to educate and empower others on matters of personal finance.

So, there I stood with the insurance check in my hand, trembling with anger, guilt, and most of all, dread. What should I do with this check? I have no idea! I have never seen, much less been the recipient of a check this large. So many zeros!

No one, absolutely no one I know would be able to guide me. I have no family or friends with significant financial knowledge. Most of my peers, like me, owe more than they make. I owe the IRS a lot of money and carry large credit card balances. If I put it in the bank, bill collectors will surely take it. Who can I trust? No one!

Therefore, I will put it away and not think about it for now, because that strategy has always served me well. You don't have to deal with things you cannot see! I can't just leave it with other mail. It may get lost. I will just put it in my purse. I fold it and put it in an unused slot in my wallet. Yes, that way it will be safe but not in plain sight.

Several months passed. I think about that check at times and then move on. There are far more important tasks to complete. I must maintain my job, feed the children, keep up the house, and try my best to move through each day.

There is almost always a sense of doom in the household. It is not verbalized but often acted out. Each child handles this grief in a different way. One is silent, one is angry, one is stoic, and one lives in terror that, I too, will be gone if I leave the house.

I decide to treat the family to a first-time-ever experience. We will go to downtown Detroit and watch the 4th of July Fireworks on the waterfront. It will be spectacular. I load them in the car, drive, park, and meander into the crowd.

We are in the middle of Hart Plaza in Detroit in 1988. There are thousands of spectators. Detroit and Hart Plaza are not known for safety and security. We walk through the crowd aiming for a spot closer to the river to get the best view. The sky becomes darker as dusk arrives.

I suddenly remember that check I am carrying in my purse! Those groups of boisterous young men increasing in number grab my attention. I see all the people walking about carrying their large cups of beer. An overwhelming sense of dread first constricts my throat, then hurts my chest.

In a moment, I realize how vulnerable I am, then suffer excruciating terror. I gather the children and tell them we must leave. I don't remember too much more of that evening, but I am sure there was some resistance, disappointment, and probably some tears.

As soon as we get home, I hide the check in a different safe place, a dresser drawer. That is how I decide to handle this dilemma. My thoughts went to that check every so often. Each and every time, I am reminded of the reality that my husband will never return home. I am so fearful of "doing the wrong thing" with this check that I continue to be paralyzed, and therefore do nothing.

After a few months have passed, I pull the check out one day while I am feeling brave and ready to move forward. I notice the date on the check and the words "void after 90 days." I count the months back-wards and an entirely new sense of dread washes over me.

How could I be so neglectful to have let that expiration date pass? I am both embarrassed and overcome with panic when I call the insur-ance company. I tell a story, probably not the truth, and a very kind lady explains they will reissue the check while advising me to deposit the new one promptly. The second check arrives and I reluctantly go to the bank and buy a CD, because somewhere I heard those are safe and earn more interest than a savings account.

As fate would have it, about six months later, my dear sister facilitated a job offer for me at a stock brokerage firm as a secretary, or sales assis-tant, as it's known in that industry. I knew nothing about the company or business, but I could type and answer phones. After all, I needed health insurance for me and my children, and this job provided it as a benefit, so it seemed wise to accept the offer.

The decision to take that job led me on a journey that I could have never imagined. Not only did I have the opportunity to learn many new life lessons, but I learned that my experience was not unique. Many women are fearful and confused when it comes to discussing money. Somehow, I determined I would help other women overcome that fear and anxiety when faced with caring for their family finances.

In this book, I have shared my insights and personal inspirations. Whether you are experiencing a financial crisis or you are seeking information to help someone else, this book is for you. You will find solutions to many issues you may be facing. I will share the good, the bad, and sometimes very ugly side of money to help you make mindful decisions about your own finances. The stories I have shared are all true. Names and some circumstances were changed to preserve ano-nymity. The stories I share about myself are all true and humbling for me in a way I hope will be useful to you.

Part One:

Dealing With Shock

Chapter One

I've Been There

You're not alone.

I know what it's like. I have felt totally helpless, lost, and terrified. I was not prepared to lose a spouse. I was not prepared to receive a large sum of money; and I certainly was not prepared to invest, save, spend or whatever someone is supposed to do with money. I have also been divorced. In that situation, I was not prepared to share debts and savings as required by law! I truly understand your fears and your frustrations.

By being willing to learn, I became empowered in my own financial situation. I believe it is my calling to pass what I have learned on to others. It is only in hindsight that I see how my journey can help others. I know now that my story is not unique. Many of us are not taught the very basics of money and finances. Oh sure, we learned to add and subtract. We may even learn about compounding interest. Did we learn how that compounding relates to our savings accounts and the reverse on credit cards? That concept alone has enormous implications.

You are not alone. There are many, many people and companies that want to help you. Most are genuinely concerned about you and have high integrity. It is those very few bad apples that spoil the financial industry reputation. Don't depend on one person. Search professional organizations, Google, and ask for references. Fear is a healthy emotion. It helps us to pause. Just don't let it paralyze you. Be brave, ask questions. Why do these people want to help and what will they receive? What is the cost to you? Everything has a price. It may be loyalty rather than dollars, just know that.

I created this book to provide basic steps for anyone who finds they're suddenly thrown into the role of family financial caretaker. While it would be better for people to learn the skills necessary for this job before turmoil strikes, most don't think to prepare, so they struggle with finding a qualified resource for help as they're dealing with some of the most traumatic emotional challenges of a lifetime. When you're facing new responsibilities while dealing with the death or illness of a loved one, it's beyond hard. In this book I offer clear, easy-to-follow steps to guide you through decisions that have to be made.

Why do I write for women?

This book can be useful to anyone but there are some unique circumstances that women endure. I learned that women generally had less money in retirement. It certainly makes sense when all the factors are considered. Women typically earn less than men in the same position. They often leave the workforce for periods of time to care for children or aging parents. Because of those reasons alone, their Social Security Primary Insurance Amount (PIA) is less than their male counterparts.

The final factor is that women are often more conservative investors. The general nature of our being is that the female of the species tends to be the caretaker and the male tends to be the hunter and gatherer assuming more risk. I am not at all stating this to be true for everyone. The gender roles today are much different than our grandparents. As society progresses, these factors are changing. I focus a good part of my business on women. I find that in the investment world, there were quite a few families in which one spouse, usually the male, managed the investments. Sometimes the female managed the household finances. It's common for a wife to reach out to me for an education when a spouse becomes ill or passes away. I want to help these women BEFORE they face an emergency. That's why I decided to host seminars, classes, and workshops to teach basic finance and especially estate planning.

Divorce rates continue to climb. Women live longer than men. There is a surprisingly high percentage of people living in poverty that are single females. When I present seminars, I ask women, "What is your greatest fear about money?" An overwhelming response is "running out" or "becoming a bag lady." These are not pleasant outcomes. We must start by building a foundation of knowledge so that we are armed for the future. Knowledge is powerful.

A man is not a financial plan. Yes, you may find someone who wants to take care of you. How nice that would feel? "Honey, I have this. No need for you to worry your pretty little mind" (gag). Don't let emotions override logic.

On the other hand, while men often may have more confidence about investing and taxation issues, they may lack experience in caretaking, medical issues, and how the house is run. It is also common for individuals take on tasks they enjoy and find interesting. These become roles of responsibility in a household over time. Therefore, this book is a resource for all who are experiencing a life event and desire guidance.

Becoming aware

Once I was introduced to the world of finance, I became compelled to continue learning. I wanted to know more about investing, economics, and all aspects of personal finance. I was intrigued to find that money brought up different emotions in people. Many people used money as a means to survive. Others used it as power for manipulation. Do you know anyone who has a spouse that insists on reviewing the grocery receipts when she shops? I have known several women in that situation. That dominance led to emotional and then eventually to physical abuse.

I learned that money caused anxiety for some and brought joy for others. I learned that often early experiences with money define how we save or spend later in life. I would often ask a new client, "What is your earliest memory of money?" That would often trigger a very interesting conversation and also provide insight for both of us. For them, a realization of how that memory affects their spending and savings habits; for me, insight as to how I can best communicate and provide professional guidance to them in financial matters.

Coleen came to me after receiving a large inheritance from her deceased father. She was in her late forties. She looked so well put together on the outside and appeared very confident. Coleen took a seat across from me and sat upright with her hands crossed on her lap. After a bit of small talk, her demeanor softened. She told me about the inheritance and that she knew she needed financial guidance but dreaded discussing the topic of finances. She had a secure job with the state university. Her pay was automatically split between her checking, savings and retirement accounts. She used a credit card for daily expenses which was paid in full automatically each month. She preferred that I just "handle" the investments for her. As I am a believer in empowering rather than "handling," I asked a few more questions about her early life experiences with money such as her first job. She shared with me that her father had been somewhat of a bully. He had been a dentist in a solo practice. He'd hired Coleen to help in the office when she was fifteen. Each Friday when he handed her a paycheck, he demanded she sign the check over to him so he could fund her college savings. She recalled hearing him mutter, "She is not worth the money I pay." No wonder she was reluctant to discuss money. This early experience led to several issues around money in her adult life. She rarely looked at her bank statements. She always abdicated financial decisions to someone else. She admitted that discussions about financial planning made her physically ill.

Through listening to her story, though, and developing an understanding of what prompted her issues with money, I found a way to help her find a comfortable solution. I suggested she imagine and talk about her ideal lifestyle, including the places she wanted to visit and charities she wanted to support. Coleen enjoyed a simple life without a need for material wealth. What was important to her was helping those less fortunate. Once we were able to assign dollar amounts to those goals, she wasn't so reluctant to talk about money. In fact, she became excited and engaged. Putting those pictures and goals in her mind made it easy for her to think about money management as something to enjoy, rather than dread. Today she's touching more lives than she ever imagined possible.

Advocates

I spent 25 years as a Financial Consultant at a well-respected brokerage firm. I was so fortunate to have Solange as a manager for 18 years. She was kind, understanding, and often encouraged me to step out of my comfort zone. She believed in me when I could not believe in myself.

During one of my first few years working with her, she encouraged me to join Rotary. Our office was situated in a major college town. Many of the Rotary members were highly respected professors, physicians, and alumni. After joining, I soon realized they expected me to give an introductory talk about myself. I was mortified and filled with terror. What would these professional scholars think of me? I had not gone to college and was a single working mother for all these years.

Solange assured me it would be okay and worked with me to perfect my speech. She encouraged me to be proud of my accomplishments.

She told me that my life experience was extremely valuable and that I was in a position to genuinely help others.

I gave that talk, filled with fear. Not one or two, but quite a few members let me know how impressed they were. I never imagined that sharing my story—mistakes, heartache and all—would prompt people to respect me instead of looking down on where I had been. That moment in time began to change my belief in myself for the better. I became more willing to help by sharing my story rather than hide from it due to embarrassment. I received quite a few client referrals from the members of that Rotary Club for many years to follow.

I eventually earned the Certified Financial Planner (CFP) designation. That was no easy task. Self-study during non-working hours while being a full-time single parent took me much longer than most. In fact, at one point, I moved and put the material down for FIVE years. By the time I picked it back up, many rules on retirement planning, taxes, and estate planning had changed. I basically had to start over, but I was determined and finally completed the curriculum. The final test for the designation takes place over the course of two grueling days, which includes an essay. It is graded on a curve and purposefully, only 60% of candidates pass. I was so elated when I received word that I passed. I still consider this to be one of my greatest accomplishments.

There are many reasons why you may not feel financially empowered. I will be presenting solutions to overcome these obstacles.

- Emotional: If you are going through a crisis, your emotions are often focused on the crisis and not the solution.
- Lack of Knowledge: You may feel that you don't even know the right questions to ask.
- Intimidation: You may have a high level of fear and not know who to trust. There are so many stories out there of professionals who took advantage of people in crisis.

- Age: You may feel that you are too old to learn something new like investing, purchasing large items, or filing taxes.

- Complacency: You may have become content with a spouse or a parent who enjoys making financial decisions, deferring monetary tasks to them because you do not like doing it.

Alice was an extremely intelligent woman with an MBA from Duke, but she had fallen into complacency. She had a prestigious position at a regional bank in the commercial loan department. She felt, because she worked in the banking department all day, she'd let her husband, Matthew, take care of their personal finances. He died suddenly of a heart attack at age 58. She had no idea which banks they used for saving and investing. There were no paper statements because Matthew had done everything online, and she didn't have his passwords. Of course, he hadn't intentionally kept this information from her, but neither figured she'd need to know it. Even though Alice has a keen understanding of finances, she was too emotionally distraught with grief to figure things out, so her son had to call and visit dozens of local banks to determine where these accounts were located. Alice was fortunate to have such a dedicated son — and accounts at local institutions. There's no telling how long or hard this search would have been if accounts were held out-of-state or country.

Clueless to Confident

At some point, it becomes a choice to stay in a place of comfort and security by allowing others to care for us, or to get wise and face fear with questions. Learning anything new is frightening.

My hope is to educate anyone who may someday need this for themselves, their family, friends, or clients. You never know when heartache will strike. I know how hard it is to function when you're in shock.

Preferably, you'll read this before it's urgent, but I get most don't think about such things until they're in the muck. This book can be used as a reference guide. It is not necessary to read it cover to cover. If you need a quick answer to a pressing question, this book is arranged to make it easy to find common issues and related solutions.

I encourage you, whether you're a wife, parent, sibling, or professional advisor, to do what you can to help yourself, your loved ones, or your clients understand how household money works. There are a lot of resources you can tap into on the internet, through books, and by attending seminars or classes. These range from very basic tutorials to in-depth, advanced strategies for taking care of your personal finances. You'll find a lot information in the following pages that can be applied wherever you may be in your financial journey, but don't stop there. The more you know before crisis hits, the less you'll need to devote precious energy and brain space to finding things or figuring out where your money is coming or going.

I share my story in this chapter, not to brag, but to illustrate managing your finances is within your reach. If I can go from an uneducated, widowed, single mom with no clue about any of this to a CFP® and daily money manager touching thousands of lives, anyone can be successful in their quest to conquer financial literacy. The first step is often the hardest. Take that step and you'll find liberation awaits. It is my goal to provide you with clarity so that you can look beyond the daunting tasks that you are facing. Ask questions and be curious so that you gain understanding. Take control with a piece at a time. Small steps will keep you moving forward. Leaping forward is great but not always practical or even possible. Once you have clarity and have taken some control, you will feel more confident. This is a process. Allow yourself time and courage to ask for help when needed.

Chapter Two

First Things First (Shouldering Grief)

When faced with a crisis, our primal instincts kick in. We feel an urgent need for fight, flight or freeze. I personally prefer flight. Can't I just go to sleep or leave town and come back when all of this is resolved? How can I possibly get through this? There is too much to take care of.

This chapter will provide some insight on how to first realize your emotions while understanding what you're feeling is common. These instinctual reactions serve a purpose for self-protection. You're not alone.

If you're a loved one of someone who's experienced loss, information in this chapter will help you better understand what they're going through. While you can't know what they're feeling, having a better grasp on grief behavior can help you be better support.

Shouldering the Shock

If the money is coming because of a spousal death, family death, or divorce, you are engulfed in a variety of emotions. Here are a few examples that I have either experienced or helped another person navigate:

Sadness

This, of course, is one of the first emotions and will take form in many different ways over time. If the loss is sudden, it will not seem real right away. This is often our bodies and minds stepping in to protect us.

Some people are very open with emotions. Others, like me, tend to hold everything inside. It sometimes looks like you are just fine to the rest of the world. Even the smallest tasks can prove to be unbearable.

I remember unloading the dryer and not knowing what to do with my deceased husband's clothes. I had a complete meltdown. After all, it had only been a few days ago that he was wearing these. Did I share that with anyone? No, it seemed so petty at the time. The smell of someone lingers long after they are gone. Sights, sounds, smells and touches are all likely to bring on a sense of desolation.

Guilt

This emotion again shows up in strange places for some of us. Memories of senseless arguments provided a great catalyst for me. Why didn't I…? Endless memories of selfish actions brought on self-condemnation. Discarding objects that I had complained about now brought a sense of guilt. There was that stupid-looking cowboy hat with a giant feather. It was atrocious, ugly, and took up important space on the shelf! Now, it was going to a thrift shop. It made me smile while also feeling sad.

Another trigger may be when unexpected money comes from an insurance, inheritance, or wrongful death settlement. We may feel that we don't deserve the money and certainly, we would prefer to have the person back in our life. I was devastated when my attorney told me the dollar amount of our wrongful death suit. It was NOT ENOUGH! How could a company put a price on someone's life?

We may also feel guilt for the relief of duties if a long illness has preceded the death.

Anger

This too may come quickly, "Why them?" One moment I was sad, the next moment I was angry. It may take a while, but chances are, it will surface. My youngest son was six when his dad passed. It was three days before his birthday. It took me years to realize why he was so withdrawn, angry, and never really happy on his birthday and the weeks leading up to it. The day my husband passed was also my oldest daughter's 16th birthday. We had actually celebrated the evening before, for which I was so thankful. Birthdays for her have carried tremendous stress and sometimes anger.

Denial

This can also be a very powerful, protective emotion. For the sake of my children, or so I thought, I would move on as best I could. It often felt very normal to resume regular activities. Other times those activities would bring up anger and grief in me and the children. It's so common, I've certainly gone through this, to expect the person to walk through the door or make that long overdue phone call. I would recall storylines from movies and soap operas in which there had been a mistake and the person did not really die. Why couldn't that happen with him?

Acceptance

The timeline for this is also extremely different for each person. If the decedent had been ill for a while, it may take less time because you may have already gone through some of the above stages during the illness. My readers may think that the loss of my husband was recent due to my recollections. In fact, it was over 30 years ago. It has taken me that long to put these thoughts on paper.

A Plan for Coping

Quite a few coping strategies were suggested to me. The few that I actually applied truly helped and included:

- Keeping a journal
- Starting new traditions, especially for holidays
- Writing letters to the deceased letting them know everything, good and bad

In addition to all of these mixed feelings, new financial responsibilities will absolutely arise. You may need to pay bills, renew insurance, or decide whether to buy or lease your next vehicle. Just taking the vehicle in for service and maintenance can be daunting. You may become the breadwinner and primary tax filer in the family now. You may need to take over the role of grocery shopper, meal planner, and taxi for children. If it is a parent that has passed, you may need to assist the surviving parent with the duties that the deceased spouse handled.

I strongly encourage you to find resources and people to help you with these new responsibilities. No one should ever be expected to handle all of these tasks alone. Section Four of this book will provide information and resources so that you can enlist the help of others and build teams.

Chapter Three

What is a Daily Money Manager?

When it became time for me to step away from a corporate position, I explored my options. I still wanted to help others, especially women, with their finances in a very personal way. I had witnessed dilemmas that my clients faced as they aged. Not only loss of a spouse but cognitive decline, mobility issues, and especially being a target for scams and exploitation. I explored the idea of becoming a daily money manager. In this role, I would be able to provide ongoing financial services and oversight at a very personal level. Little did I know how much more I would learn and how emotionally connected I would become with families and their finances. Money is very personal. Statistics tell us that most people would rather discuss almost anything with their children other than money.

A daily money manager is a person or small company that assists individual and families with daily financial tasks. The tasks may include picking up, sorting and reviewing mail, reconciling bank and credit card statements, paying bills, organizing files, setting up systems for organizing papers, gathering documents for tax filing, negotiating with creditors, preparing financial statements, assisting with spending plans, and oversight of accounts to monitor for fraud. They may also help with payroll of household employees, assist an executor through the probate process or even be named as the legal power of attorney.

A daily money manager is not a well-known resource. This was one of the many reasons I chose to start a business focused on this need. I had spoken with a couple of people in my area that were already providing this service. I then attended the National Annual Conference of The American Association of Daily Money Managers. I took the Basic Business Course to learn how to get started. The organization is small relative to other financial groups. All the attendees were very collaborative and truly had a passion for helping people.

The organization has a website, www.aadmm.com, where you can search for local money managers, read helpful articles, and find resources available for the general public. To become a member, a background check is required by a third party. This provides another level of security for the customers of members.

Traditionally the personalized service of stepping in to pay bills and monitor accounts for someone has been done by a family member. Due to people starting families later in life, having full time careers, and parents living longer, a sandwich generation has evolved.

These adult children may not always have time, expertise, or the interest to step in to care for aging parents' financial tasks. They may not live in close proximity. The aging parents know that their adult children are busy and often don't want to burden them. The children may not even realize that their parents need help until some catastrophe occurs.

People that could benefit from hiring a daily money manager are those who need assistance with paying bills, keeping up with mail, or organizing finances. If the financial caretaker within the family becomes ill, begins to have cognitive decline, has sight or writing difficulty, passes away, or just becomes uninterested, this can be an extremely valuable service. Several of my clients have adult children who live out of state so I have been able to assist them and report to the distant adult child if the client desires. I have found families to be genuinely appreciative and supportive of my services.

I was called in to help Evelyn, a mother of three adult children, keep up with the bills when her husband passed. Although dad had cancer and had been going through treatments for several years, he only let his sons know he was terminal two months before he died. These sons all had families and businesses of their own and were living out-of-state.

Clearly, his illness had affected his ability to keep up with his usual financial responsibilities. We discovered that he had not filed taxes in three years. I jumped in to help resolve that issue as well as many other financial tasks that had fallen through the cracks during his illness.

After a few months working with Evelyn, I started to suspect some significant "forgetfulness." She often misplaced bills and checks that we were expecting in the mail. As I kept her sons updated, it was easy for all of us to attribute this to stress. Eventually, it seemed prudent to get her to her doctor for testing. Imagine our surprise when we discovered she had had several small strokes. She was hospitalized and moved to a memory care facility close to one of her sons.

The sons didn't notice the progression of her memory loss when speaking to her on the phone. It was my reports and resources that led to this course of action and ultimate diagnosis; one they were all very grateful for as we discovered the why. They tapped me to step in and complete the time-consuming process of getting the house cleaned out, repaired, and listed for sale. This was done seamlessly with the group of outstanding professionals I had already vetted. Evelyn's family is extremely appreciative for having a daily money manager to lean on.

Much Needed Service

A daily money manager may also be a resource for people who have limited knowledge, interest, or time to keep up with ongoing financial tasks. People who travel extensively or have more than one residence to keep up may want someone else to monitor that utilities, taxes, and maintenance fees are paid on time.

I am able to assist executors when a person has passed. This can be extremely overwhelming. Some of the tasks may include changing names on financial accounts, utilities and credit cards. There may be property that needs to be disposed of or cleaned out. Insurance forms need to be completed and filed. Final expenses need to be paid and there may be an estate tax filing requirement. If the executor lives out of the area, the burden is compounded.

A daily money manager may have extensive knowledge in medical billing and filing of insurance claims. They may be a notary or at least have access to one if needed. They may be able to serve as legal power of attorney, legal financial guardian or conservator of an incapacitated person. As with any professional, you should be willing to ask for references, experience, education, insurance they carry and cost of services.

As many others in this business, I have an extensive list of other professionals to provide services that are not within the scope of my ability or expertise. I work only with professionals whom I have vetted and obtained references.

As a daily money manager, I am also available to help individuals and families develop spending plans (budgets). I am often called in to assist with or improve savings and spending strategies to align with a client's resources. There is an additional certification available for daily money managers who have worked in this capacity for at least three years, passed a written test, and maintained ongoing continuing education.

Part Two:
Gaining Clarity

Chapter Four

Common But Confusing Financial Terms Explained

Don't feel bad if all the financial terms being thrown at you by advisors, family, or friends leave you scratching your head. It might seem overwhelming at first, but these numbers are easy to understand when you stop thinking about them as figures and start recognizing how they apply to your life. The following pages provide simple explanations and illustrations to help you see what these terms mean.

I'll also show you how the numbers impact your life. While these words are prevalent in the financial industry, they're foreign to lots of individuals trying to get a handle on household cash flow issues. It's normal to think this stuff is too complicated for you to understand. It's not.

The problem is, most who have been doing this stuff for years, or decades, forget the early learning challenges. That makes it overwhelming for someone trying to follow language that's foreign. This chapter will help you get clear on terms, numbers, and cash flow strategies that are important for you to know.

Accounts

Types of Accounts

Checking/Savings: Usually held at a bank. These accounts may or may not earn interest. The money is readily available. You may be charged fees for a number of services such as paper statements, overdrafts, check copies, or ATM withdrawals.

Brokerage: Held at an investment firm. The account may be able to hold stocks, bonds, mutual funds and cash, money market investments, or even CDs.

IRA: Individual retirement account. This is a type of account in which you put a portion of your earned income before taxes. When you withdraw the money, you pay tax. This is often referred to as a "tax deferral." If you withdraw before retirement age, which is age 59 1/2 as of this writing, you may also be subject to a tax penalty in addition to taxes. An IRA is an account, not an investment. You may choose the investments within that account. Other types of retirement accounts are 401(k), 403(b), SEP, and others. I would recommend that you understand what type you may have and why.

Again, these are only the very basic. There are also special account types for minors, or others who cannot legally sign or understand account documents. A reputable financial advisor will help you determine the types of accounts that are best suited to your circumstances.

Investments

Types of Investments

Money Market: a type of savings account that often refers to the holding as shares. Each share is usually valued at $1, but in reality, they could be worth less than $1.

CD/Certificate of Deposit: You are basically loaning your money to the bank. They, in turn, promise to pay you back on the "maturity date" and add some interest. There may be a penalty if you need to cash it out before the maturity date.

Bond: Another way for you to "loan" your money and get some reward (interest) in turn. The type of bond indicates what institution you are loaning money. US Savings Bonds and US Treasury Notes are issued by the US Government. They are considered the safest investment because the US can always print money to pay its debt. They also pay the lowest interest. They have a maturity date (when you get your money back) and stated rate of interest. A corporate bond is issued by a corporation. They will generally pay a higher rate of interest but if the company goes out of business, they may not be able to pay you back. A municipal bond is issued by a municipality (city, county, state) and is backed by that taxing authority or through a stream of revenue like a toll road or bridge. Bonds often may be sold before maturity but will have a value that is based on current interest rates rather than supply and demand.

Stock: Stock represents ownership in a company. The ownership is represented in "shares." The company may be private or public. If the company does well, your stock shares will likely increase in value as more people want to be owners. If the company does poorly or goes out of business, your shares could become worthless.

The above-mentioned investments are only the very basic. Another entire book could be dedicated to investment language. My objective is to not overwhelm you with terminology. I would encourage you to only invest in what you understand. If a professional tells you that it is not necessary to understand the investment, walk away. If you cannot explain the very basics of your investment to someone else, it may not be appropriate for you.

Chapter Five

Insurance 101

You will likely need to look over some of your insurance policies, especially when a spouse dies or when you're facing a divorce. The role of any kind of insurance is to TRANSFER the financial risk from you personally to the insurance companies.

Health Insurance

This may be the most important insurance to have. If you are not covered by an employer group policy, consider engaging an expert to guide you through the many choices. The lowest payment is rarely the best value overall. Other factors to consider are co-pays, deductibles, co-insurance and maximum out-of-pocket charges.

Let me explain the terms you're most likely to encounter:

Premium is what you pay, usually monthly, to the insurance company. If you have insurance through your employer, they may pay a portion or all of the premium.

Deductible is the amount that you are responsible to pay before insurance starts paying. The higher the deductible, the lower the premium in most cases.

Co-pay is the amount you are responsible to pay on each claim/visit even if you have already paid the deductible. For example, if you have a $20 co-pay and the doctor visit is $200, you pay the first $20 and the insurance pays $180.

Co-Insurance is similar to co-pay but it is stated in a percentage rather than a dollar amount. It often applies to larger claims and does not take effect until after the deductible is paid. Typically, you may see the designation 80/20, which means the insurance pays 80% and you pay 20%. Of course, this could result in a substantial out-of-pocket cost for you on a high claim. A hospital stay or surgery costing $50,000 would leave you owing $10,000 before insurance kicks in.

Out-of-Pocket Maximum means that once this amount is paid by you, including deductibles, co-pays and co-insurance, the insurance company will pay all costs. Once again, the lower this amount (your share), the higher the cost of the premiums.

If you do not have employer insurance, often referred to as a "group policy," you may need to obtain insurance on your own. Healthcare. gov is the resource for that (as of this writing). Registering your choices through this site often entitles you to subsidies and tax benefits you can't get when you buy a policy from a broker directly. If you are eligible for Social Security or over 65, Medicare.gov will be the best resource to get started.

There are professionals that can assist you in navigating your choices. Some are representatives of a specific insurance company and some are independent. An independent may represent several companies. They are usually paid by the companies they represent when they sell you a policy. Therefore, there is no out-of-pocket cost to you for the consultations. Just be aware that there may be additional insurance policies available that they are not presenting to you. That is not a negative factor, just a fact that you need to recognize as a consumer.

Auto Insurance

This should be purchased by anyone who owns a vehicle. At the very least, most states will require you to carry PL & PD. This is Personal Liability and Property Damage insurance. PL & PD protects you if you are at fault and damage property or injure or kill someone while driving. Your insurance company will cover victims' costs of items such as property repair, lost wages, and pain and suffering. Each state may have different laws regarding the type of vehicle insurance required and what is covered. You may hear the term "no-fault" which means insurance pays medical without regard to who caused the accident. It is extremely important to have such coverage in place. The personal liability coverage, also called bodily injury, is stated in two numbers such as 20,000/40,000. The first number is the upper limit the company will pay per person. The second number states the maximum amount the company will pay per accident. The property damage is stated in a three-number series such as 100,000/300,000/100,000. This is to cover damage you cause to other vehicles or property such as buildings. The numbers represent the maximum the company will pay per person, per accident, and maximum property damage, respectively.

Here is an example: You have the 100,000/300,000/100,000 PL & PD coverage. You are driving, run a red light and hit a car with two passengers. Their medical bills are $50,000 each. The first number (100,000) means that your insurance will pay $100,000 per person, so there is no cost to you for the medical bill. If you had only $20,000 in coverage, you could be responsible for paying $30,000 for each person's medical bills. Of course, any financial transaction would be facilitated through attorneys or insurance companies. You would NEVER just write a check without professional representation.

Let's also say their $50,000 car was totaled. Again, your insurance would cover this because you have up to $100,000 in coverage for property damage. You're also still within your per accident maximum of $300,000 (the middle number) when you combine medical costs with reimbursement for the car.

The second portion of your auto insurance is comprehensive & collision. This covers YOUR vehicle. Collision insurance will help pay the cost to repair or replace your vehicle in the event of an accident. Collision insurance will be required if you are leasing your car or have an outstanding loan on the vehicle. There will be a deductible amount stated in your policy. This is the amount you will be required to pay before the insurance company starts paying. If an accident results in $3000 in repairs and your deductible is $1000, the insurance company will pay $2000 and you will pay the $1000 to have the repairs completed. Comprehensive will cover additional items that are not the result of an accident such a theft, vandalism, or hail damage. Items such as rental car and towing may be added to your policy for a small cost.

A reputable insurance agent will help you find the policy that best covers your individual circumstances. The rate you pay (premium) is determined by factors such as your age, your driving record, the value of the vehicle, and your deductible amount. When choosing a policy, be sure you understand what is covered, the cost of the policy, and more importantly what is NOT covered. Items or events that are not covered are referred to as "exclusions" in the policy.

Homeowners' Insurance

This is required if you have a mortgage. Even if you own the home outright, you should have it, although it's not mandatory. The cost of damages from unexpected disasters can exceed the value of your home. Insurance ensures you'll have the money to make necessary repairs.

This policy will be written based on the value of your home. This will not include the land, only the buildings and their contents. Usually, coverage for buildings is based on the replacement value, which is generally different than the assessed or appraised value. There will be a deductible (the portion you pay on a claim). The higher the deductible, the lower the premium in most cases. Most policies include a "loss of use" amount, which would cover hotel expenses, for example, if you could not live in your house. Even if you do not own a home, it is a good idea to have renter's insurance to cover your personal items in case of fire or theft.

There is also a "personal liability & medical payments to others" line item. This indicates how much your insurance will pay someone if they are hurt on your property due to a dog bite, fall on an icy walkway not cleared properly, or similar incidents where someone is injured. Accidents are just that, unexpected occurrences.

You can also add high value items on as a "rider" or "personal articles" supplement. If you have art, jewelry, or family heirlooms, it is wise to discuss that with your insurance agent now. Umbrella or personal liability policies are also options to increase liability coverage if you have potential high-risk situations associated with your property. This could be a swimming pool, a dog that could bite someone or slippery steps.

Each time a new insurance period begins, you will receive a new declarations page. Ask your agent to review the terms with you. The terminology can be very confusing, so many people just file that page away without understanding it. I was guilty of that for many years until I engaged a wonderful insurance agent that made sure I understood all of the terms and what I was paying for.

Tip: You only need to keep the most recent declarations page. Shred the old one when it terminates (annually or quarterly). This is one of the items I find with almost every homeowner who wants files cleaned out. They have kept years of expired insurance declaration pages.

Life Insurance

This is meant to replace the income. If you earn an income to support others, it is likely you need some type of life insurance. You may need insurance on your life if there would be a cost to have the services you provide replaced (child care, home care, transportation, or elder care). There are many types and the choices continue to grow. Term life is usually the least costly but it does terminate after a period of time. This can make a lot of sense, though, for a parent with young kids who doesn't have much disposable income. The most important years to cover are those while the kids are still in the house.

Here is an example: You decide to buy a term policy that pays $500,000 upon your death. You are currently 30 years old and the policy cost is around $26 per month for a 20-year term policy. If you die at 40, this has been a good vehicle for you because your beneficiaries receive $500,000 and you have paid $3120 in premiums. If you live the full 20 years, you will have paid $6240 total but did not have to use the death benefit. Not dying is a good thing. The peace of mind that comes from knowing your family will be taken care of if you did might be worth investing in a policy that may not pay anything back to you.

If you put off purchasing a term policy until later in life, it will cost more. Let's say you are now 50 and considering a $500,000 policy. In this case, the annual payment would be $1200 vs. $312 annual cost at age 30. It usually makes better financial sense to purchase these policies at a younger age.

Also keep in mind that not everyone needs life insurance. It should be purchased to cover financial needs such as support, education, and healthcare, especially for minor children. Term life insurance rates depend on your current age, health, whether you are a smoker and other risk factors. Rates are also different for males and females.

Whole life may cost more, but these policies build cash value over time. This type of insurance stays in effect for the life of the insured and pays a benefit when he or she dies. Of course, that's provided premiums are paid as required. Terms vary a lot on the different policies available, so it's important to talk to someone who can help you understand how much you're paying over time relative to what you may get back.

Annuities are a type of investment that may also have life insurance built in. These have changed a lot in recent years. Some of the newer products offer excellent opportunities for retirement cash flow with income on principal guaranteed. People more comfortable with a fixed monthly payment can find annuity policies today that make good financial sense. There are a lot of annuity products out there, though, that may not be a wise investment. Before you invest in an annuity, make sure you are clear on the fees, terms, surrender charges, and the long-term arc of payments vs. payouts.

It's really important to run the numbers on any policy you're considering. Ask your insurance agent to calculate your breakeven point. That's part of their job as your representative so you won't be charged for the service. Again, ask about what happens when you cancel or if payments are missed. It is not uncommon for policies to be cancelled for missed payments with no opportunity to get any money back that you have paid.

Other Insurance

Disability pays a stream of income should you become disabled and unable to work. This is based on a percentage, generally between 45% and 65%, of your gross income, so it doesn't always make sense and may be difficult to calculate for the self-employed.

Long-term Care provides coverage of some additional medical and custodial care when you need assistance with daily living activities (eating, bathing, dressing, to name a few). Some long-term care policies will cover the cost of home care, assisted living, skilled nursing, and/or memory care. The cost of these services is increasing substantially each year. Important factors to consider are:

- Premium: Monthly or annual cost to you
- Elimination Period: How long do you have to pay out of your pocket before the insurance company starts to pay? Typically, this is 90-100 days
- Benefit Amount: What will the policy pay? Maximum per day, per month, and lifetime
- Inflation Benefit: The coverage should adjust upwards as the cost for services rises. Keep in mind, the annual premium usually rises also

Some newer hybrid policies combine long-term care and life insurance.

Accidental, burial, cancer, and extended warranties are all types of insurance. Be absolutely clear on why you need the insurance, what it covers, expiration specifications, and limitations. These policies in particular are often sold to people who do not fully understand the terms and buy out of confusion and fear. If someone is presenting accidental insurance, ask if the payout drops when the insured turns 70. People are surprised to learn they have to continue paying the same amount but the benefit is cut in half when they turn 70.

If someone is calling or mailing you an "urgent" reminder that your car warranty has expired, call your local dealer before purchasing a policy. Your dealer or repair shop will tell you how much these companies actually pay out and how difficult it is to file a claim. These are usually not issued by the vehicle manufacturer but rather by third parties. I have spent an enormous amount of time trying to get these cancelled for clients.

You may need to engage with several different people to get the insurance you need. Never sign up at the first meeting. Do your own due diligence. Whether that is speaking with another professional, a relative, a friend, or Google, it is always wise to be knowledgeable.

 Tip: Each state has requirements and regulations that must be followed by people selling insurance in that state. You can search your state department of insurance (DOI) for more information.

Chapter Six

Account Ownership Options

During a lifetime, people open a lot of different accounts that are either solely in their name or jointly owned with others. There are multiple options for how to set this up. First, it is important to understand what the different terms mean.

Individual: This means an account has full ownership by one person.

Joint with Rights of Survivor: This is generally done with a spouse where both parties own the account in its entirety. Either person has rights to all assets at any time.

Tenants in Common: Each person owns a portion of the account. If one owner dies, his portion passes according to his will. It is not assumed or required that each owner's portion is equal. That is decided when the account is set up.

Transfer on Death (TOD) or Payable on Death (POD): This is entirely owned by one person and passes without probate to the named individual.

Community Property: Property acquired during a marriage is considered equally owned by each no matter how the asset is named. Exception is gifts or inheritances received during the marriage. Currently mandated in nine of the US states.

Custodial: An adult, the custodian, has the authority and responsibility to maintain the assets for the named minor. State laws differ as to the age or requirements for the minor to receive the assets.

Trust: A trust is an "entity" like a business. The person who establishes and funds the trust is known as the grantor. A trust document is drawn up by an attorney. The document will name a trustee who manages the assets in the trust, a successor trustee in case of death or incapacity, and beneficiaries who will ultimately receive the assets. Keep in mind the trust is just a document. Property has to be titled in the name of the trust to be managed, taxed and passed to others. That process is known as "funding the trust."

Many people are confused by all the words in just the title of a trust and how they work. This is a very common simplified example of someone setting up a trust.

Joann wants her money to pass to her children who are 12 and 14 years old. The state Joann lives in recognizes that a person who attains the age of 18 is considered an adult. They can legally sign documents and own property. Joann has a sizable stock account and does not feel her children would be capable of managing the money at 18. Her financial advisor suggested she set up a trust. Joann's attorney creates the legal document. The legal title is the Joann Smith Revocable (can be changed) Living Trust, dated January 11, 2021. Joann then goes to her bank and brokerage firms and completes forms to change the name on her accounts to Joann Smith Revocable Living Trust. The trust has now been "funded." She can also place other property and real estate into the trust by filing forms required by law. Since Joann is the trustee, she still has rights to manage the funds as she always has. The trust document may state that her children only get a portion of the assets at certain ages such as 25, 30 and 35. Be aware that the terms of the trust only apply to accounts that are put into the trust. If she does not

change the account title (ownership) at the bank and passes away, the
children may be able to receive when they turn 18.

Cautions

I want to first address common mistakes that I see with these various ownership options. These are usually just due to lack of knowledge. Even when presented with information from professionals, we often think, "That will never happen to me."

One of the most common issues I see is the titling of accounts. A person may add their adult child on an account to make it "easier" if something happens. There are so many ways this can cause future problems.

- You may have now gifted 50% of the assets to the joint holder. There are annual gift exclusions in our tax laws. Currently, a gift over $15,000 a year to an individual requires that the donor file a gift tax return. This does not increase tax at the time, but it may affect the long-range tax liabilities.

- A joint holder is an owner and has the legal right to withdraw ALL of the assets at any time.

- The assets may be subject to the creditors of the joint holder, which includes bankruptcy and lawsuits. This is not always the case but check with your attorney to be sure this won't be an issue.

- If there are multiple children, the intent may be for the funds to be split upon your death. If that takes place, your joint holder could be now "gifting" funds to their siblings. Back to reason #1, this would require another tax form if the amount is over the current exclusion. This is not necessarily a tax impact issue but something that requires tracking over time. Also, what emotional impact would there be by naming one child over another?

- If you feel that you must add someone to your account, do it with a very small checking account.

Betty inherited $1 million when her father passed away. As a new mom of twins, she was overwhelmed. Her husband, Mark, a physician, truly enjoyed investing and took pride in managing the family finances. Betty added Mark to the account holding her inheritance so he could manage the money. She never paid much attention. She fully trusted that Mark was acting in the family's best interests. It wasn't until he filed for divorce 10 years later that she learned the million dollars was long gone. She discovered he had squandered away all the money on a younger girlfriend he had kept for many years during the marriage. Betty was so distraught. Not only was she losing her marriage, she had no income or savings of her own. She was too embarrassed to tell others of her dilemma. She felt totally hopeless and helpless. Remember that adding someone to your account means they have full access to ALL of the money at any time. They don't need your permission to spend it.

TOD or POD

Another term often believed to "simplify" the passing of assets is transfer on death, also referred to as payable on death. Simply stated, the named person automatically receives the account upon death of the holder. If accounts have this designation, the document overrides any will or trust for assets to pass. The named recipient does not have ownership rights during the account holder's lifetime. This will avoid probate but may cause other problems in the estate.

My dear friend, David Huntoon, a prominent local CPA, who also holds the designation as a Certified Specialist in Estate Planning suggested I include the situation in this book. Here is why:

- If assets go directly to someone, it is now owned by the recipient. This may deplete the estate. Who then will pay funeral expenses, medical bills and taxes?
- If there are multiple children and only one is named to receive the assets, it is likely to cause family friction.
- It could be problematic to remove that person or change the account ownership later.

Banks and financial institutions are likely to recommend "transfer on death" because it is easier for the institution to process. As I have stated before, make sure you know all of the facts before you change any account title. Explore pros and cons with professionals or at least Google the issue.

Chapter Seven

Numbers to Know

Most who pick up this book likely prefer not to think about numbers and math. My objective is to make this chapter easy to follow and understand. To feel in control of your finances and gain confidence, it is important to know just a few basics. These are your numbers. As you work through gathering the information and putting pen to paper (or fingers to keyboard), you may be surprised. Your numbers will tell a story. My goal is to help you gain a sense of awareness; not good or bad, just aware.

Income

Sources of income may include:

- Salary, hourly or contract wages
- Unemployment
- Social Security
- Pensions
- Annuities
- Royalties
- Dividends and/or interest

These can be found on previous tax documents, current pay stubs, bank account records, and other financial statements. I prefer not to count distributions that may be required from your retirement accounts as income because usually those funds are just moving from one account you own to another you own. Retirement accounts are sometimes referred to as "qualified." The term refers to IRAs, 401(k)s, 403(b)s, Self-Employment Plans (SEPs), etc. The income from these is really from your own savings.

For the sake of simplicity, I would look at "take home" or net pay in income calculations rather than your actual salary as it's indicated on your pay stub. This would be the income that gets deposited into your bank or the amount on the check itself. This is what's available for spending and saving. Here are some categories you may see on a paystub listing deductions and net income:

Hours and Earnings			Taxes and Deductions	
Hours	Rate	Earnings	Description	Amount
80	$27.00	$2160.00	Federal Tax	$296.75
			State Tax	$97.38
			Social Security	$81.41
			Medicare	$28.10
Gross Year-to Date	Gross This Pay Period		Total Deductions	Net Pay
$8640.00	$2160.00		$503.64	$1656.36

You may see other entries such as 401(k) deductions, medical insurance, and life insurance. It is a good idea to look this over to understand what you are being paid and what's being taken out to pay others. This exercise alone will be enlightening if you have never spent much time reviewing pay stubs in the past.

Now we will take a look at calculating your net income. Here is an example of two quick itemizations. The first is a simplified chart for someone who is still working. Note that I did not include gross income (which is the figure before taxes and other expenses are taken out) or any of the pay stub deductions. I prefer to keep it simple at the beginning. The second chart is of someone who is now retired. It is fairly common to see a decrease of income in retirement.

Gloria's income at 48 years old (after tax)

Source of Income	Monthly	Annually
Employment Wages	$3500	$42,000
Dividends & Interest	$150	$1,800
Totals	$3650	$43,800

Karen's Income at 67 (after tax)

Source of Income	Monthly	Annually
Social Security	$1,800	$21,600
Pension	$500	$6,000
Dividends & Interest	$500	$6,000
Totals	$2,800	$33,600

I would also recommend documenting which accounts these items flow into. Are they direct deposit? What day of the month do they arrive? This will give you a starting point to develop a spending plan from your income stream. If income is less than expenses, you will need to obtain funds from other sources such as savings, additional employment, or by reducing expenses. None of these choices is pleasant to consider.

Expenses

Living expenses may entail lots of categories. It is usually easier for most to use broad classifications such as food, housing, and shopping rather than groceries, dining out, food delivery, electric, cell phone, etc. Your goal with this exercise is only to gain an awareness. You do not need an accounting degree. Don't put a lot of pressure on yourself. You also need not track every penny. Keep it simple.

Once you tally these numbers, you will have a pretty clear picture of inflow and outflow. If you determine that expenses are far more than income, we can handle that in a future step. For now, the point is for you to get a broad understanding of where money is coming and going. Here are the main and subcategories that I prefer to use.

Category	Subcategory	Category	Subcategory
Housing		Entertainment	
	Rent		Movies
	Mortgage		Theater
	Property Insurance		Club memberships
	Taxes		Hobbies
	Repairs		Sports
Electronics	Utilities	Childcare/ Education	Magazines
	Internet		Daycare
	Cell Phone		Tuition
	Cable TV		Reports
Auto/ Transportation		Shopping	
	Repairs		Clothing

	Fuel/Tolls/Parking		Home décor
	Insurance		Home supplies
	Auto Club		Shopping clubs
Financial		**Personal Care**	
	Life Insurance		Hair salon
	Tax Preparation		Nail salon
	Bank Fees		Massage
Health		**Gifts and Donations**	
	Medical insurance		Birthday
	Doctor		Holidays
	Dentist		Charities
	Eye care	**Pets**	
	Medicine		Food
	Health clubs		Vet/Boarding
Taxes		**Vacations**	
	Income Tax		Air/Train Fare
	Property Tax		Lodging

The totals for each category can be added by hand or electronically. If you are a little tech savvy, programs like MINT, Quicken, or You Need a Budget may be helpful. A word of caution: all of these take time upfront. Enlisting the help of a bookkeeper or daily money manager to set this up will save you a lot of time and possible frustration.

I set these up for my clients. The programs become smarter over time. For instance, when Verizon is sent a payment, the program assigns the expense to mobile phone. Exxon is recognized as "auto fuel." However, I have bought coffee at Nordstrom then filed it under the "coffee shop" category. Several months later, I wondered why my coffee spending was $300. It was because I bought a coat at Nordstrom and MINT assumed it was coffee again. Programs are only as intelligent as the data entry person who sets it up.

You may find it helpful to guess at each category and then enter the numbers and see how close or far off you were. Once these are set up and adjusted for a few months, it becomes easier. I can now upload transactions for some clients and categorize all of them in less than one hour per month. Sorting transactions into categories will also save you time and stress when preparing for taxes. Items that are tax-deductible such as medical and charitable will be very easy to find.

Creating your own spreadsheet or asking the computer program for totals in each category may look like this:

Category	Item	Monthly	Annually
Housing			
	Mortgage	$1,200	$14,400
	Maintenance	$ 100	$1,200
	Utilities	$ 300	$3,600
Electronics			
	Cable/Internet	$150	$1,800
	Cell Phone	$ 80	$ 960

Auto/ Transportation			
	Fuel & service	$140	$1,680
	Insurance	$100	$1,200
Health			
	Insurance	$100	$1,200
	Doctor	$ 25	$300
	Dentist	$ 60	$720
Food			
	Groceries	$ 325	$3,900
	Dining out	$ 200	$2,400
Entertainment			
	Concerts/Arts	$50	$600
	Memberships	$50	$600
Shopping			
	Amazon	$100	$1,200
	Target	$120	$1,440
Personal			
	Hair/Nails	$100	$1,200
	Gym/Yoga	$ 50	$600
Gifts/Donations			
	Birthdays	$50	$600
	Charities	$100	$1,200
Travel/Vacations			
	Air	$50	$600
	Hotels	$100	$1,200
Total		$3,550	$42,600

Cash Flow

The next step is to subtract expenses from monthly income. This number is your Cash Flow. If there is a surplus (which there is in "Gloria's income" table), you are able to put those extra funds into savings. If there is a shortfall, as there is in "Karen's Income" table, you may have to use savings to keep up this level of spending. The other alternative is to spend less. In which category can you reduce spending? This can be an unpleasant consideration and decision but a necessary one if you're burning through cash faster than it's coming in.

I don't like the term "budget." It feels too much like "diet" and deprivation. I use the term "Spending Plan," which seems to resonate better with most people.

Net Worth

The next important number to know is net worth. This is done by adding up all of your assets: savings, investments, home value, auto, artwork, etc. and then subtracting any outstanding loans such as mortgage (home loan), automobile loan, and credit card debt.

You can get an estimated value on your home by just typing your address into Google; open the Zillow or the Redfin website and you should see your home and the estimated value, which is based on recent sales in your area. Keep in mind, this number may be very different from the tax value of your home or even the actual price someone would be willing to pay. A reputable realtor can provide a more accurate value. Your automobile value can be found by answering a few questions on the Kelly Blue Book website under the tab "Car Values." If you are leasing your car, this is an expense but not part of your net worth.

Assets are property that is owned by you. Fixed assets are those items that are larger and not expected to be sold. Liquid assets can usually be turned into cash quickly to cover living expenses. Liabilities are amounts that you owe.

A very simplistic example:

Net Worth

Item	Value	Item	Amount Owed
Fixed Assets			
-Home	$425,000	Mortgage	$95,000
-Automobile	$32,000	Auto Loan	$12,000
		Credit Card	$4,000
Total	$457,000		$111,000
Liquid Assets			
-Checking Account	$4,000		
-Savings Account	$40,000		
-Brokerage Account	$200,000		
-Retirement Account	$850,000		
Total Liquid Assets	$1,094,000		
+Total Fixed Assets	$457,000		
Total Assets	$1,551,000		
Total Debt	-$111,000		
Net Worth	$1,440,000		

Assets minus debt equals net worth

Considering the above example, you could pay off the credit card debt and automobile loan from the bank savings. That is the account that has the least potential to grow. You could also pay off the mortgage if that makes sense. Often, the investments have a greater potential to grow over time than your home value so if the interest on your home loan is low, it makes sense to put your money to work earning income or growing rather than paying off your mortgage. We will review this more fully in Chapter 7.

By taking $16,000 from savings to pay off the credit card and the automobile loan, you would then only have the mortgage as a liability. Your net worth would remain the same. We just move $16,000 from the savings asset and take away the auto and credit card liabilities.

New Net Worth Statement

Item	Value	Item	Amount Owed
Fixed Assets			
-Home	$425,000	Mortgage	$95,000
-Automobile	$32,000		
Total	$457,000		$95,000
Liquid Assets			
-Checking Account	$4,000		
-Savings Account	$24,000		
-Brokerage Account	$200,000		
-Retirement Account	$850,000		
Total Liquid Assets	$1,078,000		
+ Total Fixed Assets	$457,000		
Total Assets	$1,535,000		
Total Debt	-$95,000		
Net Worth	$1,440,000		

See, isn't that easy? And you thought you would never again use that high school math. Although the car and home have monetary value, you should not count on that value to meet your living expenses. You need a place to live and probably a vehicle for transportation. Therefore, we use another figure known as your liquid net worth. Technically, this refers to assets that could be converted to cash within 48 hours. In the above example, that is $1,094,000 in the first table and $1,078,000 in the second table. Also keep in mind that collectibles like coins, stamps, and art are only worth what someone is willing to pay. That is not necessarily the same as an appraised value which is used to calculate insurance premiums or estate valuation.

A very simplistic withdrawal plan in retirement would be to allow yourself to spend 3% of the brokerage and retirement account each year. Let's use the second table after we have paid off the auto loan and the credit card. In this case, that would be 3% of $1,050,000 (1,050,000 x .03) or $31,500. For the sake of discipline, you could calculate based on December 31 value and move that dollar amount in January to your savings or checking. When you withdraw all of it in January, that would be your limit. In years to follow, the total will be different. If your investments have grown, the calculation will be a higher amount. There may be years that 3% is less than the previous year's withdrawal.

The net worth statement will be very useful for your financial planner. This is a great starting point for forecasting future money matters. A professional financial planner will help you identify tangible goals such as buying that beach house, taking a world cruise, booking an African safari, or helping family members with college costs. The plan should take into account your age and hereditary longevity.

Many of us are living far longer than our grandparents due to lifestyle changes and medical advancements. You should make it a priority to develop strategies that assume your assets will outlast your life expectancy. Many financial planners use a life expectancy of 95-100 years. We cannot predict our own date of death, but we can have an idea of how we want to live. The option of spending less now is far better than discovering you only have enough savings to live another five years when you're still healthy and active.

Credit Score

This number is only relevant for your own finances. You probably don't need it for parents or other people whom you are assisting. Your credit score is a number assigned by credit reporting agencies which indicates your worthiness or likelihood of paying back a loan. If you pay your bills on time, have borrowed, and consistently paid back lenders, your score will be higher. If you have a tendency to pay late or skip payments, your score will be lower.

There are a number of ways to obtain a no cost credit report. Some credit card companies keep this updated for you on the secure access to your account. You may also obtain this information online at annualcreditreport.com. If you happen to get to a credit score site that is requesting money, don't pay. It should be free.

You will be given a number between 300 and 850. Anything above 700 is considered "good." The score is based on several factors, including your current level of debt, history of paying loans on time, and accounts that went to collection agencies.

There are three main credit reporting agencies: Equifax, Transunion, and Experian. The score may be slightly different at each, depending on the companies that have reported your history. Do be sure to check this at some point before assuming you know what your credit rating is. You may be surprised to learn that your score is different than your spouse. It is wise to establish credit in your own name. This could be a bank-issued card, a car loan, a store credit card or even a mortgage.

Molly worked for many years and had a good salary and savings plan. She figured her credit scores were excellent. When she retired, she applied for a credit card and was shocked when she was denied due to insufficient credit history. During her entire married life, the cars and credit cards were issued under her husband's name. She was an "authorized user" on credit cards, not the primary owner! That decision meant her credit scores were extremely low due to a lack of recorded borrowing activity. She's one of many widows and divorcees I've met who are suddenly stunned and challenged by this unexpected reality.

Other "numbers" that will be helpful to know are mortgage interest rate, credit card interest rates, and debt to income ratio.

Your mortgage interest rate can deplete your savings if it's unnecessarily high. Knowing what this number is relative to current norms can help you decide if it's wise to refinance. At this writing, mortgage rates are at historic lows. If you have good credit and bought your house as recently as 2010, you may be paying more than you need to. When interest rates are low, it's also a good time to refinance a variable rate mortgage and lock in on a fixed rate which will remain for the life of the loan. This is a good time to provide a very simplified explanation of several terms you may come across when buying or refinancing a home.

Length or term: Number of years until loan is paid off – common terms are 30, 20, 15 or 10 years

Fixed rate: Interest rate remains the same for the entire length of the loan

Variable rate: Interest rate will vary and usually tied to a specific index such as **LIBOR** (London Interbank Offer Rate) You may have a very low interest rate when the loan is initiated but in the case of a "variable rate," at the end of a stated term, it will likely change. That initial period could be 5, 7 or 10 years.

Talk to your banker about options and costs. Don't forget to factor in points, appraisal fees, application costs, title search, and other costs that come with a refinance.

If you carry a balance on any of your credit cards, interest rates can run 13-24% and more. Knowing how much you pay in interest can help you decide which cards to pay off first. You might be shocked to discover those monthly minimum payments you're making only go toward interest. That means what you owe will keep going up even if you don't charge anything else to the card.

Debt to income is just as it sounds: your total debt as a percentage of your total income. This is a number that should be of interest to any company or person loaning money to you. It tells a story of how much you can afford. A financial planner or investment company you deal with can help you find these figures. I did not include these in the "must know" category because not everyone has a mortgage or debt. If you are one of those without either, congratulations!

Chapter Eight

Joy of Debt (said no one, ever)

Credit cards make it so easy for us. They allow us to shop, travel, and dine while we put off paying for what we buy. Usually, if you have not paid the credit card company within 30 days, they start charging interest. Some interest rates can be well over 20%. Remember when you thought the purchase was such a bargain at 10% off? Well, if you put it on your credit card and do not pay in 30 days, you will owe much more than that 10% you saved.

If you have a credit card with a $5000 balance which carries 16% APR (annual percentage rate) and make only the minimum payment of about $200 a month, it will take over 10 years to pay that off. You will have paid a total of $7400. Of course, that's assuming you didn't ever use the card again for those 10 years. I used a minimum payment credit calculator found on the Consumer Credit website. The Credit Karma website also has many tools and calculators. It is usually very enlightening to plug numbers into some of these calculators.

What if you have a balance owed and also now have an unexpected expensive car repair? What if you need to fly across country to care for a sick relative? Can you see the snowball effect and how simple it is to use credit? It is so easy to become drowned in debt.

How many times has a store clerk offered you a discount if you applied for the store credit card? I recently took a very informal poll asking people what they would do with $400,000 that was unexpected. Most said they would pay off debt. That led me to believe that many people are carrying debt and not feeling good about it.

I personally have had volumes of credit card debt many times. I would get a windfall, pay off the cards, and then run them up again. I had the training and education to guide others, but I often did not heed my own advice. The ability to use a credit card for instant gratification was my problem, not lack of knowledge. Looking back, I realized how I was spending money I did not have to buy things I did not need to impress people I did not like.

After many years of struggling to pay off debt because I just did not want to wait until I had enough to pay cash, I finally took the time to pay off all my credit cards, then my vehicle. Putting the extra dollars into savings and investing had the opposite snowball effect of accumulated debt. Money was growing and multiplying in my favor. The more I saved, the easier it became to save. Wow, everything I was teaching others was now working for me.

But, What About Rewards?

You may have encountered or are currently using credit cards that give you rewards. The rewards can be in cash back, airline miles or hotel rooms to name a few. These can work well but only if you are disciplined to pay the balance in full each month. You should also be aware that these cards sometimes charge an annual fee. Weigh your options. As an example, I have an airline card and build up miles. I am also able to have one bag checked, which would otherwise cost $25 each way. I pay $100 a year as an annual fee. Therefore, I must travel with checked luggage at least two round trips per year just to break even. The airline requires quite a few miles for a long flight. There may also be some limitations on dates which may be booked. Do your homework and read the fine print.

Tip: Be aware that some of the awards may be transferrable upon the death of the account holder.

No Interest?

You may be tempted to buy something or transfer a high interest credit card balance to a zero-interest card. First of all, read the fine print. If you buy on zero interest and do not make the minimum payment stated ON TIME each month for the full term, the interest will be added back retroactively for the entire term, which could be pretty hefty. That zero-interest credit card is only zero for a limited time. If you add more purchases or do not pay within a certain time period, a substantial interest rate will kick in. Also, if you transfer a balance, the card you are transferring from may charge a fee! There are many ways for credit card companies to charge fees and make money from you. I have participated in and learned the lessons on each of these.

Good Debt?

Well, maybe. Student loans and home loans or mortgages are considered good debt. One of the reasons is that the interest may be tax deductible and therefore reduce the taxes you owe. The second reason is that these loans may increase the value of what you are investing in. For instance, getting a degree could help the borrower earn a higher income in the future. I say "could" because there are always exceptions to the rule. A home may increase in value. In times like 2008 and 2009, we learned that is not always the case. Borrowing to start a business could also increase someone's net worth, but the opposite may be true if the business fails.

Another reason that a mortgage is considered "good debt" is because mortgage rates are typically lower than stock market growth over time. I will stress OVER TIME. Time meaning years, not weeks or months. If you are able to obtain a mortgage rate of 5% and your investments earn an average of 7%, it makes sense. Again, this would not be true if you bought a house in Florida in 2007 when prices were skyrocketing. The trouble would be compounded if you lost your job in 2009, then watched your investments and your house lose value at the same time your income disappeared. This scenario did in fact happen to many folks.

There are some experts who believe in having no debt. That could make life much easier but it would take years to save enough to buy a home. Renting may not be the best choice because rent can be increased at each lease renewal and you never gain equity from spending that money. Usually, when you're paying off a home mortgage, an increasing percentage of each month's payments goes toward principal.

There are pros and cons to paying off a mortgage after receiving a large sum of money. This is best discussed with a professional advisor. I would suggest speaking with both a Financial Advisor and a Tax Advisor as investment strategies proposed may have unforeseen tax consequences.

It may make financial sense to keep the mortgage if the rate is low. Once you give that money to the bank to pay off the mortgage, you cannot invest it in potentially more lucrative opportunities. On the other hand, if it keeps you awake at night thinking about money you owe, then by all means consider paying off or at least paying down mortgage debt.

My rule of thumb is to never borrow more than you know you can pay back. You should review your debt and interest rates at least once a year. As I stated earlier, debt can quickly snowball out of control.

Susan was referred to me by her adult daughter to help her get her bills organized after she discovered a large number of late payment notices. Susan had always managed the household bills. Her husband had passed a year earlier and she had recently been spending more time at home because of some physical limitations. Probably due to boredom, Susan began spending more time ordering from catalogues and TV shopping networks. She was also becoming forgetful. After several months of working with Susan, I was able to compile a list of her debt, which included 25 credit cards! She was making only the minimum payment on each, when she was making payments at all. In addition, she had been transferring balances to a new zero interest card, but then forgetting about it and using the old cards again. Her costs in late fees, interest, and penalties were extraordinary. She also opened cards to get travel benefits and/or cash back. In the big picture, this made no sense. She was paying much more to the credit card companies than she was receiving in benefits.

Part Three:

Control What You Can

Chapter Nine

Protect Your Assets

There are many different ways that people can attempt to take your hard-earned money. I'm going to break these down into categories on how shysters may contact you.

There will always be people who feel entitled and will take from others. This can happen through scams or fraud. It might be a stranger, but more often, it's a friend or family member who has gained your trust. Take the time to think through any situation. Do not give money or sign contracts based on fear, urgency, or pressure. If it doesn't feel right, just pause. Here are some red flags to consider:

1. You feel an urgency to act due to a phone call, email, or in-person meeting
2. The person won't give you time to call others
3. They ask for payment with gift cards
4. They ask you to pay before work is complete
5. They ask for a blank check or your credit card information before work is completed
6. They make you feel foolish when you ask for clarification
7. You don't fully understand what you are paying for or to whom

In Person

First, there is the longtime successful scam of pickpocketing. This may involve more than one person. One person distracts you by getting your attention and another may grab your purse, wallet, or other item. A slight variation on this is when someone appearing very innocent asks for your assistance. It could be helping them find a lost dog, retrieving dropped items, or anything else to gain your immediate trust. They may then provide a very sad story requesting your financial assistance. First, they earn your trust, then they ask for money.

Phone

This is nothing new. There are two types of scammers to be aware of here. First, there is the person who will play into your caring emotions. They have sad stories and convince you that you can make a difference. If it's a charity, do NOT give your information over the phone. Ask them to mail or email information. Once you receive documentation, check charity verification websites such as Charity Navigator or another reputable third-party agency for legitimacy, tax deductibility and ratings.

The other emotion people play upon is fear. Fear certainly arises when we believe that we or a loved one is in danger. It may be someone posing as a grandchild that is in a hospital or jail. It may be someone claiming to be an IRS representative, a police officer, or another authority getting ready to arrest us. If you get a call like this, take a deep breath. Allow your thinking to move to the logical side of your brain. Ask questions to be sure you are speaking to a grandchild such as "What is your dog's name?" If they claim to be with the IRS or law enforcement, ask for their ID # so you can verify their identity before sending money. They will most likely either hang up or become very rude to you.

Some scammers may tell you that you have won something and first need to pay a tax. Again, do not send money or give your information over the phone.

Social Security and IRS employees will NOT call you. These agencies send letters by mail.

Your credit card company may call, but they will never request you to give them your password, username, or other personal information. If they suspect fraud, they will read off a couple of previous transactions and ask you if they are legitimate.

ANYONE, I REPEAT, ANYONE that requests payments in the form of gift cards is not legitimate.

One of my current daily money management clients, Kate, received a call from a very nice man who claimed he was from Medicare. He told her that she should NOT use the paper card that she received in the mail because he would be sending a new plastic one for "security" reasons. To do so, he said he needed to verify her Social Security number, date of birth, and mother's maiden name. She had just gotten that new paper card, so she assumed this was a legitimate request. As I was reviewing her mail the following week, I asked her about a letter verifying her online access to the Social Security Administration. She typically did not use her computer other than for email, so this was a red flag. There was another letter sent a few days later verifying a change of address. We immediately called the Social Security Administration. It took over an hour to start the resolution process. She also had to go in person to the Social Security Office for additional verification and reporting requirements. The next step for the perpetrator would have been to set up direct deposit information for the monthly checks. If he had succeeded in getting this far, it would have been extremely difficult to recover the money. I later learned this is becoming a common scam.

Mail

A common mail solicitation that also sometimes comes by phone is offering extended warranties on your home, car, or appliances. These are not sent by the manufacturer. They are sent by third parties in bulk (which is why there is no stamp on the envelope). Shred the ones you receive in the mail. In fact, you can shred almost anything that comes in a postage paid bulk mail envelope (no stamp).

A check from "winning" or "qualifying" to win something is usually not legitimate. Don't deposit it in your bank. It will bounce, you will be charged a return fee, and now the perpetrator knows who you bank with because of the way the bank marks the check when they process it.

While on the subject of mail, I would suggest using a locked mailbox for outgoing mail that contains any personal information. Think about this; you make out a check to pay a bill and put it in your curbside mailbox with the red flag up. You are telling the world that there is something in that box. Take a quick look at a check you would mail. What type of information could someone obtain if they picked up that envelope out of your box? This becomes a much easier way to obtain your information that going through the trouble of trying to hack an online account.

Email

Many scam artists are now using email. It costs the perpetrator virtually nothing to email, unlike phone or mail scams. Do not click links (underlined in blue) in any email! If you get any, hover over or right click on the sender's address at the top of the email. That will usually confirm that it is not really from the company or individual mentioned. I still get the ones saying they are a long lost relative or have "found" a substantial sum of money and want to share it with me. When I check the sender's address, I see something like XXXXXX@ gmail (dot com). I have gotten emails that appear to be from banks, credit card companies, and shopping sites. When I hover over or right click the sender's email address, I notice what comes after the @ is not the address of that institution.

Here is a sad case that happened to a client of mine:

Bob was on his computer and got a popup notification that his computer was infected. He was prompted to call a number on the screen. Now Bob is 78 years old, extremely intelligent, and has a lifetime of business knowledge and common sense. He had been having some computer issues so he followed the directions and called. A very polite young man answered and took him through some steps. Bob could not locate the correct program, so the young man offered to do it for him. Bob allowed him access. It all happened so fast. Yes, he gave him access to his computer, then soon realized that this young man could now see all of his files, accounts, and additional personal information. Bob quickly hung up and shut off his computer. He was extremely worried but also embarrassed. He called his daughter who then stepped in to help. She had to spend an entire day off work calling all the banks and companies he dealt with to close existing accounts and open new ones. All passwords had to be changed too.

Predators

Anyone who takes your money for their own benefit is a predator. They may appear to be kind, authentic and caring. They are often, however, self-serving, focused on putting their desires first. Predators can be found anywhere but are not easily recognized at first.

The term con-artist is derived from the word "confidence." The first step for any con is to first gain your confidence. They do this in a number of ways. I have known finance professionals that looked for potential new clients by reading obituaries and death notices. They would then call the widow to express their condolences and build trust over time.

The internet is filled with information people can search to find potential victims. Recent home sales are public knowledge. They are easy pickings for someone selling "home warranties" or other home services. Graduations, births, marriages, deaths, and divorces are all opportunities for insurance sales. Lawsuit and lottery winners are vulnerable to investment "opportunities."

Predators can live in your neighborhood, attend your place of worship, and belong to the same organizations and clubs as you. They will use those connections to build the trust. This is not to say that everyone is a predator, but just be aware. Be cautious of whom you share personal information with.

One of the most common victims is a person who is lonely, perhaps socially isolated. Online dating can certainly pose a threat. It's easy to make a false profile to gain the confidence and trust of someone.

I actually had to testify in court against a man who was on trial for murdering his wife. She was an extremely talented musician but very introverted with few friends. The gentleman had courted her and married her while he was married to another and also dating several women across the country. All of this was, of course, unknown to her as his job required a great deal of travel. This wife had been reported missing for months and was eventually found dead in a local lake. He was arrested for forgery after he had drained all of her accounts and ran up the credit cards. I was asked to testify regarding falsified documents. He had created checks on his home computer that appeared to have been issued by the firm I worked for. He was found guilty. That forgery became the motive for murder. Another one of his previous wives had been killed by a hit-and-run driver who was never found. It makes you wonder how much murder practice he'd had before he got caught on forgery. He is now serving several life sentences.

Unfortunately, family members are among the most common predators. Elder financial abuse is more prevalent with family members than strangers. It may begin very innocently. Sharon is checking in on Aunt Ruth several times a week because Ruth is starting to forget when to take her medicine. Sharon starts going more often and decides not to take her annual vacation because Ruth may need her. Ruth gives Sharon her credit card to buy household items and Sharon starts using it for her personal purchases, at first by mistake, but then with frequency. Sharon feels obligated to check in daily and begins to feel that she deserves compensation. Who will know?

An adult child may be having financial problems and decides they should get their inheritance now while it is most needed. If there are siblings, this can cause additional family conflicts.

I have seen tragic results when a daughter is expected by a parent to take over the financial duties. She feels incapable and subsequently turns over mom's finances to her husband. Hubby claims to have expertise but in reality, he sees this as an opportunity to try his luck at investing in some risky day-trading. It does not take long for the money to "evaporate." Of course, the daughter feels mortified when she finds out, and soon the siblings are no longer on speaking terms.

Patrick suffered a stroke after his only son passed away. His wife had died six years prior. The couple had amassed enough money during their lifetime to ensure Patrick's care needs for life plus having plenty left over to pass on to his only grandchild. Amanda, his daughter-in-law, would visit Patrick several times a week and bring his five-year-old grandson,

Chayton. Amanda seemed to be a loving and kind-hearted daughter-in-law. She would bring cookies and other treats for Patrick and help with his bills. This included writing out checks that Patrick would sign and mailing them. I was brought in when Patrick's attorney suggested he hire me to help organize documents for tax preparation and also keep an eye on cash flow. Amanda was directed to put all bills and statements in a box for me to pick up and review. I noticed the bank statements were missing starting several weeks after Amanda began her visits. With online access, I soon discovered many substantial checks written to Amanda. She claimed they were to reimburse her for supplies and food. Patrick was also paying her a salary and her credit card balances each month on top of the checks! On the advice of legal counsel, I took over paying all bills and set up a system that made future disbursements to Amanda require receipts. Patrick refused to accuse her of any wrongdoing because he did not want to give up seeing his grandson. Amanda still visits but her "personal income" was decreased by about $10,000 a month once proof of expenditures on Patrick's behalf was requested.

Chapter Ten

Loans and Gifts

Receiving a large sum of money has additional drawbacks that can affect relationships with friends and relatives. For me, money was another tool that I could use so that people would like or accept me. I have loaned and gifted money for that reason several times. Fortunately, I was usually paid back.

I encourage you to think through any and all requests for loans from well-meaning people. You have a right to determine how your money is spent, saved, or invested. This right can also be a burdensome responsibility. You have the power to control your financial security.

Gifts

Gifts in their true nature are given with no expectation of reciprocation. If you are generous in nature, or just have a big heart, you may want to gift to those less fortunate. I would advise caution in making such decisions. Make sure you are gifting for the right reason. It's also important to confirm you can afford to give the funds away. It may seem as though you have plenty now, but really take the time to weigh this with your trusted advisors. What impact will this gift have on your finances later? If you give to one relative, will you feel obligated to give to others also?

Many people want to share their newly acquired wealth with others.

I was called in to help Sarah set up a spending plan. When her hus-band had passed away, she received $1,000,000 from a life insurance policy. She paid off debt, including the mortgage on her house, with the funds. The rest was dwindling quickly as she bought a large, very expensive dog. His diagnosed heart problems escalated the cost of care. Sarah wasn't working and didn't plan to but took her two children and their spouses on a very expensive vacation. A million dollars feels like a lot of money, and it is. The spend down of that amount is the important number. You see, by the time I met her she had $450,000 left and was planning another vacation. Almost half of the $1 million was gone within the first year. If she continued to spend at that rate, the money would not come close to lasting her lifetime. She was 45. Curiously, even with that burn rate, she did not think she was overspending. I sus-pect this was a way to help herself through the grief. I totally understand that. For many years of my life, I lived by the motto, "There are still checks in my checkbook." That was a very dangerous game for me. I helped her devise a spending plan that was realistic for her age. After several discussions in which she gained some clarity, she also said she would consider working part time.

Don't forget that if you are planning to share this wealth with people, be sure to check with your tax advisor. If you are making gifts for more than the "exclusion limit," a gift tax form may need to be filed. That is not saying the gift is taxable, but the form is required.

Loans

Providing a loan to someone means that there is an agreement in place for the funds to be paid back to you. If you are making a loan, I would strongly suggest that you have the terms of the loan put in writing. Depending on the amount and complexity, you may need legal sup-port. Alternatively, it may be a simple transaction. If the terms are not followed and the loan is not paid off, it could be considered a "gift" for tax-reporting purposes.

Remember in either gifting or loaning, it becomes difficult to say no once you have provided funds to someone. One more suggestion I would make is that when approached to provide a gift or loan, consider saying, "Let me check with my advisors first." That may relieve you from having to say no and causing the requestor to feel hurt or resentful.

Often, the funds you have received were meant to take care of your needs first and foremost. The plan may be to ultimately pass to children and grandchildren. In my experience, most spouses bought life insurance so that the surviving spouse would be well cared for.

Co-signing Loans

Another word of caution: If you co-sign a loan, you are agreeing to pay it back if the primary borrower cannot for ANY reason. I have seen this situation many times. A common scenario is believing, "This will never happen to me." Whether it is a close friend or relative, proceed with extremely high caution. Here is a scenario I witnessed:

Peter and Wendy are dating and plan to marry. Peter has been going to school and driving a car that his parents bought so he has no credit established. Wendy has excellent credit and has been gainfully employed for the last four years. Peter wants a new vehicle because he just got a fabulous new job. Wendy co-signs for the $35,000 loan payable over 60 months (5 years). A year later, the engagement gets called off. Peter gets laid off from his job and moves out of state with the car. Even though Wendy does not have the vehicle, she is responsible for the payments for the next four years. Missed payments also go on her credit report. This would be a great case for Judge Judy if she could locate Peter.

Of course, co-signing a loan may work out well when you can help someone establish credit. I helped several of my children in this way. As with outright loans, I would suggest that you consider worst case scenario when co-signing a loan.

Chapter Eleven

Ready or Not; Ready is Better

This chapter is written to provide some guidelines for anyone who has to step in as a financial decision-maker due to a life event. This event will often be sudden and unexpected. Emotions can be your enemy when dealing with money. Most of us have a rational, logical part of our brain to help with tasks such as writing, calculating, driving, and puzzle solving. We also have an emotional side which produces the fight or flight response. Fear, anger, joy, love and sadness can lead us into making decisions for the wrong reason.

Each of the scenarios I have listed – death of a spouse, death of a parent, divorce, or stepping in to care for someone experiencing sudden illness or hospitalization – have some similar steps. Some of the items that will be true for most of the scenarios is the need to:

1. Arrange for child and/or pet care
2. Arrange for an alternative mailing address or request a mail hold
3. Discover and stop any automatic home deliveries of supplies, food, newspapers, etc.

Death of a Spouse

The death of a spouse is one of the most stressful life events. The extreme grief of losing a life partner can be devastating. Add to that, the surviving spouse now has to assume more responsibilities in the family in addition to ones they have done in the past.

Roles that I suddenly had to assume were overwhelming. I was now the breadwinner and head of the household. I now had to arrange for home and auto repairs, which I had never done, on top of my usual duties of shopping, cooking and laundry. I know this sounds archaic in some ways, but I believe that most couples split up household tasks over time and division of those duties become a normal way of life. Taking out the garbage cans would bring out an underlying anger as I mumbled, "I hate this" and other times, I just sobbed. Don't even mention shoveling snow, which goes on for months where I lived.

Here are some tasks that will need to be completed following the death of a spouse. The first three are most urgent. The remaining can be done over weeks or even months.

- Notify friends and relatives, estate attorney, and employer. Ask others to help with calls. People will often want to help in some way. Some friends and family may do this from your home so they can also accept calls and visitors for you.

- Arrange for burial, cremation and/or funeral service. A memorial can take place at a later date if that makes more sense. A funeral director can be referred by a friend or minister. Flowers, preferred charities, and obituary language and placement are all decisions to make. Once again, allow others to help with these challenges.

- Notify Social Security. It's common today for the funeral home to make that contact and arrange for death certificates, but double check. Request at least ten certified copies. Financial institutions, insurance companies, the Department of Motor Vehicles, and other organizations the deceased has done business with may request certified copies.

- Locate any will, trust, or other estate documents. Review safe deposit box locations and contents.

- Notify life insurance, financial institutions, credit bureaus, credit card companies, and Veteran's Association.

- Keep receipts and statements for all expenses. Retain all statements for the month that the person passed. You will need those for tax preparation.

- If you were a joint holder on an account or a beneficiary, call those companies first. If the account was in the name of deceased only, the estate attorney can advise on next steps. You may need to be appointed by the court to be executor and will be given Letters of Appointment.

- Notify auto insurance, home insurance, loan companies, and utilities to get spouse's name removed from accounts.

At this point, I want to throw out some cautions. If some ongoing charges, such as utilities, insurance or cell phones, are being billed to a credit card in the name of the deceased, the card may get closed and those bills will not get paid. It's very important to review recent statements for automatic charges. You may need to change the billing, which can be another daunting task. The same advice goes for checking accounts and automatic payments. Some banks will automatically close accounts when they receive word of a deceased client. Others may allow you to retitle the account in your name and continue payments. These several tasks are one of the main reasons that I suggest having no more than three financial institutions.

Next steps should be to review any online accounts and close them, if possible. Having a password manager or access to a password list will make this a much easier task. Magazines, newspapers, and gym memberships will all need to be cancelled unless you want to continue paying. Upon reviewing client statements, I will often find recurring charges to old memberships and publications that have not been used in years. It does take time and patience to get these stopped, but they often add up to more than my monthly fee.

I was recently working with Rose whose husband had passed a year ago. She sold an office building they had owned soon after he passed. Nine months later, I came across an annual insurance bill for that property. Rose had not cancelled the insurance, unaware that she should have done so. I called the insurance company, provided the proof of sale, and she was issued a refund check in the amount of $500.

Going through a crisis can easily make us forgetful. Another reason to have trusted professionals is to assist in sorting out paperwork and other details. Other family members could be helpful but remember, they may also be grieving and under undo stress.

Death of a Parent

The death of a parent can happen at any point in our life. It is never a pleasant experience. Whether it is sudden or has been expected due to an illness or accident, we are never quite ready to say goodbye. I feel fortunate to have had my mom as long as I did, but I still miss her every day. She was 75 when she passed and had been suffering physically for a relatively short time. My dad passed at 85 years of age. Losing my parents was a reminder of my own mortality. Being the oldest child and knowing that I was now the Matriarch of the family was a sobering realization.

When a parent passes, adult children often have to step in to settle an estate. If there is a surviving spouse, their kids may also have to take on some of the duties of the absent spouse, at least for a short time. These responsibilities often fall upon the child that lives the closest. It is also often a female.

In my case, it was my sister. She stopped by to see my dad several times a day after my mom passed. She brought him dinner, sometimes lunch, and set up his weekly medicine doses as my mom had done. She was also working full time and had a husband and two sons to care for at home. I'll note it right here publicly that I am so very grateful for the time and support that she provided during her own grieving.

Due to my own experience and time spent with families I have worked with, I have put together this checklist of tasks that need to be completed when a parent or other close family member passes away.

- Notify other family and friends. Enlist their help to notify others.
- Contact local funeral director and/or clergy to arrange for service, burial, cremation and obituary.
- Notify employer.
- Arrange for child and/or pet care.
- The funeral home will usually notify Social Security and prepare death certificates. Ask for at least 10 certified copies.
- Notify estate attorney. Someone will be expected to act as executor or administrator. This is determined by the will, if there is one. The attorney will then arrange for Letters of Administration to be prepared by the Clerk of Court. This task can be taken on by anyone but it does take time and some understanding of the probate process.
- Notify financial advisor, banks, credit unions and health insurance carrier.

These tasks can be very easy if the decedent was organized and prepared. If not, it could be a very daunting task to locate information that will be needed. You will need to:

Locate the original will, and/or trust documents.

You may need to obtain marriage license, driver's license, military discharge papers, property deeds and time share deeds.

You'll also need bank statements to determine what income was being received and if it was in the form of checks or direct deposits. Each of those income sources need to be notified. Pensions and Social Security payments should stop on date of death. If money was sent after that, it will need to be returned. Also, any income after date of death should be put into an estate account. You will need to obtain an Estate Tax ID to open a bank account in the name of the estate. There may be exceptions to this depending on the size of the estate and state laws.

Bank statements will show expenses that are paid each month. Some may be paid automatically; some may be by check or bill pay. These may need to continue to be paid. Look for transactions such as mortgage, utilities, credit card and insurance payments.

Locate insurance policies and file claims including ones with an employer. Claim forms can often be found online or requested by calling the insurance company. I suggest keeping copies of claims or written correspondence until payouts are received.

Close or update ownership on bank, credit card and investment accounts. Be cautious of closing accounts that are receiving direct deposits or have automatic payments going out. If the accounts are closed before those companies are notified, it will double the work you have to complete.

Notify utilities to change owner and payment method if necessary. This step may not be mandatory but may save time in the future if the surviving spouse moves or changes banks.

Notify credit reporting agencies and the Department of Motor Vehicles. Look for recurring transactions that may need to be cancelled such as Netflix, Hulu, club memberships, Amazon Prime, magazine subscriptions, and vacation clubs.

Most of these responsibilities fall upon the executor or surviving spouse. If you don't have the time, patience, or expertise to perform these tasks, you may want to hire a daily money manager, paralegal, or other qualified professional. My clients are usually more than willing to pay me so they do not have to take time from work or family to complete these. I have found it is much easier to open accounts and GIVE companies your business than it is to close them. Most of the notifications have to be handled either face-to-face or via phone. There are very few that can be completed entirely online or by mail.

Divorce

A divorce is also likely to create a financial dilemma combined with overwhelming emotions. There will most likely be times of anger, guilt, fear and sadness. These feelings may be accompanied by joy, relief and liberation. There may be times that you feel all of these within a short period of time. Be assured that you are not alone. I personally have been through divorce and worked with many clients trying to navigate the challenges.

You may have family, friends, or a supportive attorney to provide guidance. Here are a few tasks that I suggest you complete sooner rather than later.

- Retitle or open new bank, investment and credit card accounts in your name only. You may be tempted to add an adult child, but please do not. That can be extremely detrimental down the road no matter how capable or trustworthy they are.
- Change or update beneficiaries on all life insurance policies, retirement accounts and annuities, including those that are provided through your employer.

- Update your own estate plan including will, trust and power of attorney.

- Update ownership on automobiles and property that may not have been mentioned in the divorce decree.

- Contact companies holding your policies and change the name of the owner on home and auto insurance. If you have to file a claim, you probably don't want the insurance payment to be made payable to you and your ex!

- Let your financial advisor, tax advisor, daily money manager and estate attorney assist you in these matters. This is especially important if you have little time, knowledge, or interest in taking on these tasks.

Eileen was going through a divorce after a very long marriage that included nurturing kids now grown. She had spent her adult life raising the children and volunteering. Her husband owned a very demanding business that kept him away from important family moments. Eileen had always paid the household bills, handled all the shopping, arranged for car maintenance, organized travel plans and managed home repairs. She was the COO, or Chief Operating Officer in the household. While going through the divorce, she realized that she needed help with understanding the investments, estate plan and tax issues that had always been the responsibility of her husband. She knew she needed a team of professionals to guide her through all the documents and changes that needed to be made. I built a professional resource cohort as part of my role as her daily money manager. As we worked through the changes, I made sure she thoroughly understood each step of the process and the reasons for recommended changes. She's now empowered and confident in financial decision-making. This new knowledge and attitude led her to decide to sell the large family home. Eileen is now renting a house near her son and first grandchild. She's been liberated with the realization she can spend time with family knowing her finances are in order and designed for her benefit, resulting in a newly discovered financial freedom.

Once you survive a divorce, you'll discover you now have additional life choices. Choose your professional and personal support team with care. They should always put your best interests first. Family can be a great support system, but they can also be a hinderance. Don't allow or rely on someone to make all of the decisions for you. Allow yourself the freedom to learn and become empowered.

Hospitalization or Illness

More often than death or divorce, a sudden illness of a loved one may require that someone step in to help with financial tasks. This may include paying bills, depositing checks, and keeping up with correspondence. Although this may be a temporary situation, it still requires time, energy and some expertise. Some of the steps mentioned below are required.

- Secure care for children and pets.
- Notify employer, family and friends. Recruit help.
- Gain an understanding of income sources and how money flows into accounts.
- Review statements or files to determine what expenses are owed and how bills are paid.
- Arrange for mail pick-up and bill paying.

Even though the situation may be temporary, having a plan of action and assistance will allow loved ones more time to focus on the patient.

My dear friend, Liz, was scheduled for a medical procedure last year in mid-December. Complications arose and she had to stay in the hospital for several weeks, which was not her plan for year-end festivities. She recruited me to help her because she was worried about month-end bills that were due and tax obligations. I was able to review her mail and keep all of her bills and taxes paid. Her adult children were able to focus on her and she was relieved to know the tasks were being completed. I continued to help for a few months after she got home so that physical recovery could be her priority.

Chapter Twelve

Managing Finances for Others

In my experience, it is becoming more common for people (spouses, children, or a professional) to step in gradually, over time, to help with finances. As we age, there are many reasons why we may need help with daily tasks such as finances. It is often difficult to turn over these tasks to someone else. We experience many losses as we age: friends, family, health, hearing, eyesight – just to name a few. Very often, an aging person is asked to stop driving due to slower responses and poor vision. That can be devastating. Giving up control of the checking account or bill paying is just one more loss that some people will struggle with. It is often an adult child who will step in.

Here are a few signs that may indicate someone needs some help in keeping up with financial matters:

- Growing stack of unopened mail
- Receiving late notices, account closure letters, or utility shut off threats
- Reluctancy to discuss money or mailed items
- Confusion over accounts and credit cards being used
- Change in normal behavior such as spending, gifting and charitable contributions
- Rushing to answer the phone whenever it rings

If any of these behaviors are new or seem to cause anxiety, it is certainly worth discussing. This is a time in which aging adults are more susceptible to fraud and scams.

Sudden Illness

When you are suddenly faced with stepping in as a financial caretaker, it can be an immense undertaking. If your "person" was very organized, it will be easier. That is often not the case. If they use online access to manage their finances, it may be fairly easy to step in if they provide access to you. If not, there are some time-consuming tasks that will need to be completed.

Need to Know

Income Sources

If employed, the employer will need to be notified. A representative at the company may be able to provide additional information about medical, disability and life insurance available.

If retired or not working, are there unemployment, government, or Social Security benefits being paid? Is the person receiving any pensions, Veteran's, or annuity payments?

Assets

An accurate accounting of all bank, credit union, investment, and retirement accounts should be compiled. This will not only provide a picture of resources for expenses but will also be needed for Medicaid claims and for some alternative medical housing qualifications. If there is a safe deposit box, where are keys and who is authorized to access it?

Power of Attorney

You may already be named as a legal representative for the person. If not, you may need to get the legal appointment. That will usually require an attorney and the ill person's authorization. If they are unable to communicate, it becomes a more difficult task and may require a court to appoint a legal guardian. Most financial institutions have additional forms they require to allow anyone other than the account holder to access accounts. Each company has its own process. This power of attorney task can be exhausting.

Bills/Expenses

Once you have access to the financial accounts, you will need to determine how bills come in, how they are paid (check, automatic, bill pay) and from which accounts. Some may be paid by credit card. This can usually be determined by reviewing recent statements from banks and credit cards. Reviewing the utility bills, for example, will rarely give you information on how the invoice is being paid. The utility bill may have Auto Draft imprinted but no indication of the account that is paying it. If the payer is receiving bills by email and you are unable to retrieve their email, this again will add substantial time and energy to getting the bills paid.

Insurance

Attempt to locate all insurance policies. These should include:

- Medical, including supplemental if on Medicare
- Long-term Care
- Life Insurance
- Disability
- Accidental and/or cancer policies
- Veteran's Benefits
- Auto, Home, Personal Property

It is wise to review the beneficiaries, if the person has not passed, making sure they are up to date and accurate. If the beneficiaries listed are no longer alive or no longer desired, updates should be made as soon as possible. This is a critical task that could result in big challenges if it's not taken care of before someone dies or becomes unable to communicate.

I was recently helping Jack, who is 96 years of age, with organizing his files so that I could help his wife if he became ill or passed. I came across about ten small life insurance policies that he had purchased from friends over the years. Upon further inspection, I found the beneficiaries on each to be a trust that had been dissolved 20 years prior. The trust had named a bank as the trustee. I helped him get each of those updated to pass to his wife, adult children, or grandchildren. It took time, patience, several phone calls and the completion of forms, but I guarantee that is now one mess the children will not have to untangle.

Chapter Thirteen

Tackling Mounds of Paper

One of the greatest stressors for most people I have met with is the never-ending stream of documents. This chapter will help you determine what to keep, then how to keep it organized, plus how long records should be archived. You may also want to explore ways to reduce hardcopy material being sent through the mail. This is a task that can be very time-consuming on the front end.

If you are comfortable, set up statements and reports to be emailed. Websites such as the Federal Trade Commission Consumer Information site provides information on resources to stop junk mail, including pre-authorized credit card and insurance offers. Alternatively, you can call each company that sends you catalogues, subscription offers, charitable requests and other mail you do not want. Emailing these stop requests may put you on an email list that adds to your document clutter, so proceed with caution.

How long do I need to keep this?

That is the ultimate question when trying to keep papers and records organized. I would like to start with the easiest first. If you are hanging onto deposit slips, ATM receipts, grocery receipts, gas receipts, etc., ... don't! Most of these items can be verified the same day by logging into your bank or credit card account. If not, once they show up on a statement, shred or destroy them. They are taking up valuable space in your drawers, purse, countertop, or car cup holder. If you are saving receipts to help you create a budget, there are easier ways to accomplish that.

Once you receive a utility bill and confirm the company recorded last month's payment, destroy last month's bill unless you need it for a business expense. Most utilities have online access that allow you to review old statements if you are curious. Once you have full trust in the system, you may even change to paperless statements and auto bill pay. I would, however, remind you to keep the access to that company site documented in a password manager or a list you maintain with all your User IDs and Passwords in case you (or someone) need to cancel, change, or update the account.

- Insurance policy "declaration pages" for previous years can be destroyed once they are no longer in effect. You will see a "term" date at the top of the page.
- Vision prescriptions usually expire after one year, at which time they can be tossed.
- Product warranties can be disposed of upon expiration.
- Receipts for large ticket items such as televisions and computers may be kept until the warranty is expired.
- If you did not deduct your auto insurance or your pets' boarding cost, no need to keep those receipts.

Lifetime of owner

These documents should be kept in a place free from water, insects, or extreme heat. They may be difficult, costly, or time-consuming to replace.

- Birth Certificates
- Death Certificates
- Will or Trust (only the most up-to-date one)

- Power of Attorney for Medical and Financial Agent (only most up-to-date)
- Social Security Cards
- Original Insurance Policies
- Divorce Decrees
- Adoption or Name Change Documents
- Military Discharge Papers
- Pension Documents

Hold only until year end summary or tax document arrivals

Receipts needed for tax filing should be kept in a file or separate box. This will make preparation for you or others easier at tax filing time. I like to keep a file or large envelope for each year that contains a copy of the tax return along with documents, statements and receipts of items listed on the tax return. Each item may have a shorter holding requirement than the actual tax document, but to keep it simple, keep all in one envelope.

Income: If you keep pay stubs, you can discard these once a W-2 is received. Because most companies will report year to date income, it is not necessary to keep any but the latest or last pay stub.

Dividends, investment sales, interest and withdrawals from retirement or tax deferred college savings accounts statements can be kept until the 1099s are received. These will usually arrive in January or February. The envelope generally states that it contains tax forms. The titles of these forms will be somewhat intuitive such as 1099-INT for reporting interest, 1099-DIV for reporting dividends, and 1099R for reporting retirement withdrawal income. Once you have the 1099, you may shred monthly statements, but there is also no harm in keeping them for several years if you have the storage space.

Contributions to retirement plans: If you have made contributions to an IRA with after-tax money, the amount will be needed for your tax return. After tax means you take it out of your own bank. If your employer subtracts income tax, Social Security and Medicare tax from your pay, the amount you receive is "after-tax." If you invest some of your remaining paycheck in an IRA or other tax-saving option, keep records of all payments until after the tax return is completed for that year (due in April the following year).

Medical expenses paid out of pocket: This includes long-term and medical insurance premiums that you pay after tax. Many hospital and doctor groups now use a system that you can access online to pay your bills as well as review or print the totals that you have paid out of pocket. Your pharmacy will print a total of your annual spending on prescriptions. You may also choose to keep receipts, credit card statements, or bank statements but you do not have to keep duplicates. I encourage you to use a system that is easy and makes sense for you. Just remember that if anyone has to step in and help, easy is better than complicated or duplicated. These payments may be deductible on your tax return, so it's important to keep track of them.

Tax Payments: This includes real estate taxes, payments made to IRS or state for income tax and personal property tax. Personal property tax in some states is paid with your annual vehicle registration. Other jurisdictions may have their own invoice.

Real Estate Interest: This is interest you pay on a mortgage. You will receive a tax document. It also shows up each month on your mortgage statement. You need not keep each monthly statement, especially once you receive the mortgage interest and annual property tax statement. You need to keep this for three years after the due date of the return showing the deduction.

Charitable donation receipts: Donations made by check or credit card should be kept separate from in-kind (clothing, household items) donations. Currently, the IRS requires a receipt from the organization for any donations over $250.00.

Business, rental property income and expenses: Keep these receipts until you have an itemized annual summary.

Your tax advisor will provide more guidance based on your personal situation and current tax laws. Both of these may change more often than you realize.

Keep for three to seven years

As of this writing, the IRS website states that taxpayers should keep tax returns and back up documents for three years, but there are several exceptions. The exceptions are based on the year you paid the tax that was due. To be safe, I usually recommend clients hold onto records for seven years. Ten is an easier number to remember, so some prefer that. Keep in mind that if you did not file or filed a fraudulent return, the required retention for tax return purposes is indefinite.

Hold until sold or transferred

- Property deeds including time shares
- Membership contracts including vacation clubs
- Original loan documents
- Automobile/vehicle titles
- Loan documents and promissory notes should be kept until paid in full or sold.

Once paid in full, keep the letter stating it is paid off.

Receipts for property or items you have purchased that you may sell at some point should be kept to prove the cost, especially if they increase in value. This could include real estate as well as art, jewelry, coins, antiques and collectibles. For instance, if you bought a piece of land for $5000 and sold it ten years later for $10,000, you have a gain of $5000. This is called a capital gain and is taxable (currently at a lower rate than income). If you did not have that original purchase receipt, the IRS may assume that you paid zero and that your gain is $10,000. Of course, you could always get that original record from the County Clerk, but there lies the issue of cost and time spent to retrieve it.

The receipts for other tangible items are important not only for resale but also for insurance. If you had a fire or theft, it would be extremely helpful to have receipts for those valuables. Many items decrease in value after purchase such as everyday automobiles, boats, household appliances and the like. It is not necessary to keep those original receipts unless they are under warranty. Even most owner's manuals can now be found online, so those can be tossed if you choose.

Memorabilia are usually irreplaceable. Pictures and some documents can be scanned onto computers or flash drives. If you truly enjoy touching and seeing certain objects and pictures to reminisce, try to pare that down to one or two boxes over time. Professional organizers and downsize specialists are often very helpful. They are experienced at helping people decide what objects truly spark joyful memories. They are also helpful in finding good homes for special items. I recently helped clear out a house and learned that a local animal shelter was thrilled to have the old towels and blankets.

As you are purging items either in an ongoing fashion or all at once, be cautious as to what goes into recycling or trash. Any document that has your name, address, phone, or account numbers could end up in the wrong hands. Separate those items to be shredded. A good practice is to keep a small shredder near your garbage or desk and shred junk mail as it comes in. If you prefer, you can take a box or bag to a local office supply or packaging center to shred on site. If you have boxes or bins full of papers to be shredded, there are on-site shred companies. They bring a truck to your home and shred in your driveway while you watch. Keep in mind, this would not be cost effective for a few boxes because you are paying more for the truck and driver.

Another service available are junk haulers. They will pick up almost anything from your home. Some of these companies specialize in keeping items out of landfills so they will do their best to recycle or repurpose your junk. They also charge by the truck so it makes the most sense when there is a large accumulation.

File Guide

Set up a file system that makes sense to you so that you will use it. You will need to retrieve items for the following situations:

Tax filing, buying or refinancing a home, personal loans, estate planning or settlement, divorce, applying for financial aid, or Medicare.

If you are very visual, you may prefer to see all of your files. This can be done with a vertical type file organizer setup. I use clear acrylic so that my clients can see all of the folders. Because they are standing vertically, the files take up less desktop or shelf space.

If you prefer to have an uncluttered desktop, hanging folder systems may be more appealing. If you don't have a file drawer or cabinet, you can use a plastic, metal, or cardboard file bin. The folders can be hung and the bin can be placed in a closet or cabinet.

If you prefer to go paperless, utilizing a computer and scanner may be a better solution. You can set up folders, sub-folders, and even sub-sub folders. You can label each as you would in hard copy methods.

Make a daily habit of putting all of your receipts and mail in one box, tray, or bin. Keep a shredder and recycle bin nearby to dispose of junk mail as it enters your home. If you lack the time or discipline to keep up with this, I suggest hiring someone to keep your filing up to date. If that box becomes full and/or gives you anxiety, it is usually an indicator that you need assistance. This process will alleviate stress at tax time or whenever you need to locate a document.

Karen provides home care for her ailing husband. He had always han-dled bill paying and tax organization. Caring for him is now her 24/7 job. When she eventually hired home care assistance after doing it alone became too daunting, they suggested she bring me in to help with papers, bills, and taxes. By that time, she referred to the home office as her "dreaded room." Now, the mail and papers she does not understand go into a "Teri" box. Karen doesn't see her office as a dreaded room anymore. She now only uses it to handle tasks she's comfortable with, so she enjoys the space again. Wouldn't it be great if we could all just dump our stressors into a delegation box? She constantly tells me how relieved she is to have me on her team. Sometimes the answers to improv-ing quality of life are simple.

Here are some ideas for main and sub-folders. Everyone's house-hold is different so use or add only those that are applicable to your family.

- **Income**
    Wages, Employment
    Interest, Dividends
    Social Security, Pensions
- **Financial**
    Banks and Credit Union Statements
    Brokerage Statements
    Retirement Accounts

- **Insurance**

  Life, Disability

  Home, Umbrella

  Medical, Dental, Vision

- **Medical**

  Receipts or Paid Bills

  Prescriptions

  Health Reports

  Immunization Records

- **Taxes**

  Real Estate Tax

  Personal Property Tax

  Estimated Tax Payments

- **Debts**

  Credit Cards

  Education Loans

- **Home**

  Mortgage Payments

  Services and Repairs

  Homeowner's Association

  Utility Payments

- **Automobile**

  Repairs and Service Records

  Insurance

  Loans

- **Family**

  School

  Clubs and Memberships

    Subscriptions

    Hobbies

    Family History

- **Travel**
- **Pets**

    Health Records

    Training

Have you noticed these categories are very similar to the ones I listed in Chapter 6? Those items needed for taxes can now be easily found. Having a system that works for you will enable you to feel more in control.

Chapter Fourteen

It Takes a Village

No one succeeds alone. That doesn't just apply to work or family life but also in dealing with grief. The team you put together ahead of time or during crisis is there to help you. Knowing you have people to lean on will help you get through this. Getting clear on what you can lean on them for will reduce confusion and stress.

Coming into sudden wealth is not always a blessing. You may have heard stories of people winning the lottery or receiving a large inheritance only to see it dwindle away after only a few years. Why is that? There are a number of reasons. It could be lack of knowledge, poor decisions, being overly generous, or being taken advantage of by others. One of the reasons for this book is to pass on my knowledge and experience to help my readers keep the money that they come into. It could be an inheritance, insurance payout from a death or an accident, winnings from a lottery, a divorce settlement, or even a retirement account that has been accumulating for years.

There are probably numerous people out there ready to help you. I have asked previous clients what they felt was the most important thing I had provided as their financial advisor. The widows and divorcees overwhelmingly agreed that it was the professional team that I helped them put together. They felt the people that I trusted and introduced to them were invaluable.

This team should all be people that you trust, who are working for YOU and are willing to talk to each other. I add that last point because your professionals should be able to collaborate so that nothing is missed in your financial plan. You also don't want duplication or services that do not complement each other. A friend or relative that offers to provide several of these services at a low cost or no cost may be a RED FLAG.

Some questions you should ask any professional that will be working for you or your family are:

- How long have you been in your current role?
- How often will we meet?
- What services will you provide and what are you unable to provide?
- What differentiates you from others in your field?
- How do you bill and how much should I expect to pay you?
- Will you provide at least two current client references?
- Why are you in this profession?

I would suggest that you interview at least two people in each profession. Pay attention to how the person makes you feel. Will you be intimidated or feel very comfortable to share your personal information and ask questions?

Estate attorney

Everyone has an estate plan. It is either decided by you or by state laws. If you have a will, a trust, or have named beneficiaries on accounts, that is part of your estate plan. If you have no will, trust, or named beneficiaries, you are said to have died intestate. Each state has a specific set of laws that determine who is to receive your estate. Those procedures must be followed and may not have been what you wanted. This pertains not only to your assets but also who is named guardian of your minor children and who will sign all documents and pay creditors on your behalf.

An estate attorney will create, review, and/or update your legal documents such as a will, power of attorney and/or a trust. Upon the death of a loved one, they will guide you through the probate process. At the very least, you will need several certified copies of a death certificate and a certified letter from the court appointing an executor or administrator to legally take care of the decedent's affairs. An estate attorney will help you navigate through this process. You may choose to obtain these on your own through the Clerk of Court without hiring an attorney. That may save money but will cost time and possible frustration if you are not knowledgeable about these matters.

As your financial situation changes throughout life, you should review your legal documents. Any time there is a significant change in your circumstances or tax and estate laws, your estate plan should also be reviewed.

Always name a contingent beneficiary. If your primary beneficiary passes and there is no contingent (2nd option) named, the payout will go into the estate. Estates are taxed at a higher rate than an individual.

Mary's retirement account had her husband, Bill, named as her beneficiary. He died, leaving Mary too busy and overwrought with grief to remember to change her beneficiary to her married son, John. She died six months later. Now her beneficiary is deceased, with no contingent beneficiary named, so the account is paid into the estate as a retirement distribution. The estate tax rate today is 37%. Had it passed directly to her son, whose tax rate is much lower, at 22%, there would have been a lot more money left after taxes. He could have spread the distribution over several years (up to ten as of this writing), which would have meant even more money going to him instead of the sizable lump sum paid to the tax man.

Don't assume that your wealth will be passed to your spouse or children automatically. It is imperative to have your desires written out in a legal document. If you move out of state, you should have a local attorney in your new state (or country) review your will to ensure it complies with the rules in place where you now reside.

Assets in which you name a beneficiary such as life insurance, pension, 401(k), IRA, or annuity will ALWAYS pass to the person you have listed as a beneficiary. Wills and trusts DO NOT override any financial asset that allows for a beneficiary. Many people are surprised to learn this. You must take steps to change the beneficiary if you no longer wish to leave an inheritance to them or if they pass before you do.

Mary and Bill divorced. Bill forgot to change the beneficiary listed on his life insurance policy offered through his employer when their marriage ended. He got remarried, and still forgets to make a beneficiary change. When he dies, Mary, his first wife, will get the insurance money even though they are divorced and his new wife is his intended recipient. Don't be Bill.

Yes, you can prepare documents from online services and save money up front. It may seem like your estate is simple and it's not worth paying an attorney to develop a smart estate transfer plan and prepare your will. That may well be the case but it is highly unlikely! It may cost your heirs more to undo a poorly executed plan. Life is filled with uncertainty and changes. A reputable attorney trained in estate planning is well worth the cost in the long run.

On the flip side, you may have a fairly simple estate and not need a sophisticated plan. A simple situation may be that you are married. All assets you own are jointly held with your spouse with rights of survivor, or you have listed beneficiaries AND you only own property in one state.

Here are some issues that would require a more thoughtful and extensive estate transfer or trust plan (and associated professional guidance):

- Real estate (including deeded time shares) held in several different states. Even if you have a will, probate will be needed in each state upon the death of the survivor (if jointly owned).
- Child with special needs who will require care after parents are deceased.
- Second, third (or more) marriages, with children from past marriages.
- Desire to pass on assets privately (probate court makes everything public).
- The state you reside in has a high probate cost.
- Desire to specify when and how much heirs receive over time rather than providing a lump sum at age of majority (18 in some states).
- Planning for incapacity. A will only determines asset distribution upon death. A trust will allow you to specify who can act on your behalf if you cannot speak or are not of sound mind.

There may be additional circumstances in which a trust may be advisable, but of course, the best way to determine if these apply to you is to talk to a professional skilled in estate planning. Some attorneys may offer an initial free consultation, so it's usually a good idea to schedule a conversation.

Financial advisor

A financial advisor will be the person you see most often and on a regular basis when money transfer and money management issues arise.

Therefore, this person may be the leader of your professional team. You may already have a financial advisor and/or financial planner. If not, you will have many choices and probably many referrals to people in this line of work. They may work for a large firm or be independent. There are pros and cons to each of these models.

A large firm may have many internal services, specialists and products. They may also offer banking, insurance and home loans. They often have a toll-free number that you can call at any time. There are usually a number of people that you can interact with. This may be very efficient but it also might feel impersonal at times.

A small firm may have more autonomy and more personalized interactions. Although they are not available 24 hours a day, they might have more flexibility to meet on your terms, even if that is out of state. An independent advisor may be a Registered Investment Advisor (RIA) or fiduciary who doesn't sell insurance or home loans. They will, however, be able to introduce you to those other professionals if needed.

Whether you prefer a large or small firm, it is best for you to hire an advisor who operates in a fiduciary capacity. That means that the advisor must put the needs of the client ahead of his or her own compensation. They cannot recommend an investment simply because it has a higher commission or referral bonus for them. They must recommend the most appropriate solution for the client's objectives and circumstances. The advisor should have a thorough understanding of your goals and financial situation as well as your willingness and ability to take on investment risk. Yes, every investment has a risk. Keeping money in a savings account is safe but will not keep up with the rising cost of goods and services (inflation). Even leaving money under your mattress carries the risk of fire or theft.

I personally recommend that your financial advisor have a Certified Financial Planner (CFP®) certification. This designation will require that they work as a fiduciary. You may see lots of letters after someone's name on their business card. Each of those requires thorough knowledge, experience, testing and continuing education. Never hesitate to ask someone what the acronyms mean and even why they obtained them.

Some people are comfortable working with several different firms. If this is the case for you, I would suggest not using more than three, including your company retirement plan. This will prevent duplication of investments, will ensure appropriate alignment of your resources, and most of all, make it much easier for someone to take over in the case of illness or death.

Whether you are choosing or changing financial advisors, there are many resources for professional qualifications information. Even if your advisor comes with a strong recommendation from a friend or family member, I suggest you do your own due diligence. You want to make sure that they are registered with regulatory agencies and currently in good standing, with a respectable track record. Here are a couple of respected regulatory agencies:

FINRA Broker Check

This resource indicates if a person or firm is licensed to sell securities and/or offer investment advice. It will even provide a list of people who have been banned.

Securities Exchange Commission (SEC) Check Your Professional

As part of this agency's independent federal government regulatory responsibility for protecting investors, this SEC listing provides registration status, backgrounds and judgements or court orders issued against financial providers. This applies to formerly registered professionals too. Even though I am no longer practicing in selling securities, you can look me up and verify my history.

CFP Board

This website (CFP.net) can help you find a Certified Financial Planner.

While there are other regulatory agencies and organizations, they're not as well known or comprehensive as those I mention. These are the first that I would recommend you search.

Tax advisor

A tax advisor will help you sort out tax issues and determine the most efficient way to file taxes as they become due. In the case of a death of a loved one, there may be several tax returns that need to be filed. Other cases such as inheritance, divorce, the sale of a business, retirement, or windfall financial gains should be reviewed by a reputable tax advisor. It is always better to get smart, professional guidance before the funds are spent, loaned, invested, or used in other ways.

You may find that some people are able to provide more than one of these services. It is wise to check their credentials and ask for references. Convenience and specialized experience are factors to consider. An attorney may specialize in estate planning and have also obtained a Certified Financial Planner™ designation to expand their knowledge. A Certified Public Accountant may also have earned a certification as a divorce planner.

I once met an accountant that also sold mutual funds. She did not have a background or experience in providing investment advice but boasted that her clients tell her everything so it was easy to sell them funds which provided her with an additional source of income. I personally would not recommend a person with this mindset as a credible advisor.

There are many types of tax advisors. It can be confusing to search for one if you're not clear on what you need. Levels of expertise can range from bookkeeper to accountant or Certified Public Accountant

(CPA). The education, state licensing and certification requirements are different.

A bookkeeper needs no credentials or specialized education. An accountant is not necessarily certified. They may have additional education in the area of accounting and maintaining financial records. A CPA must pass an extensive test covering accounting, business concepts, tax laws and regulations. They then must document continuing education to maintain the certification.

An Enrolled Agent (EA) is a resource that is not commonly known to most people. This professional usually has a tax background as a CPA, accountant, or has been employed by the IRS. They have extensive training with federal tax law. They have the ability and training to represent taxpayers with the IRS. This can be a substantial relief for a client who is facing an audit. I can tell you that receiving a letter from the IRS is a very frightening experience. These professionals can be found by searching the National Association of Enrolled Agents.

What is the Cost?

This is a very good question and one that I hope you will ask often. It is also important that you understand, not just hear an explanation or read a disclosure. Everything has a cost. Everyone has to make a living. You should know how each of these professionals are paid. Reputable professionals disclose how they are paid. These professionals should be able to provide you an estimate of time that will be needed for the services you need. Typically, the more education, accreditation and experience, the higher fee you should expect to pay. It is harder to predict tax or legal service hours because the more digging you do, the more complicated the unknown situational circumstances may become.

Sometimes a person is paid to provide a service by their employer such as a delivery driver or store cashier. A portion of what you pay for goods pays their salary, right? Some employees receive part of their income from their employer and part from customers in the way of gratuities such as food service staff and hair stylists. Most people understand these concepts.

It becomes a little less clear in the financial service industry. Some financial professionals may charge an hourly rate. Some may charge as a percentage of your assets they manage, often referred to as fee-based. Others may be compensated by the companies whose products they sell to you. Each of these has pros and cons. It is most important that you understand how your cost is determined and charged to you. Be very skeptical when services or products are offered at no cost.

Financial advisors are held to the standard of suitability. That means they should only present investments to you that are suitable for your circumstances. Age, income, length of time to invest and net worth are all "suitability" factors. There could be a conflict of interest if the advisor recommends a product that pays a higher compensation to him in the way of upfront fees, commissions, or other incentives.

A fiduciary standard takes that determination to a much higher level. As stated in the previous section, a fiduciary is required to act in the best interest of the client. You should always feel comfortable asking if your professional is a fiduciary.

Cost vs. Value

You will see a common theme as you browse the topics in this book. We can't have a discussion about money without mentioning value. What is value? Value is the benefit you receive. There is likely a cost to obtain the item or service. Always be very aware of the cost and what you will receive in return for that cost. The lower cost item may provide less customer service. It also may be a lower cost because your representative is being paid by someone else, like another company intending to sell their product or service to you. If that is the case, be sure the item is the best fit for you. You should never hesitate to ask why they believe this is the best for you and what alternatives are available. You should always have a full understanding of the product and perhaps even be able to explain it to someone else.

The lowest cost service may not be the worst and the most expensive may not be the best. Be aware of what you are paying for. In my case, you would be paying my hourly rate for the years of experience and knowledge as well as my exceptional client service. You may hire someone for a lower hourly fee because you just need a bookkeeper. That is truly fine. My clients will tell you that I understand their estate plans, can discuss tax exposure with their CPA and can recognize potential fraud. I also keep family who live out of state updated, as necessary, on their parents' health and mental state.

Health Care Team

Life-changing events are likely to bring on stress and/or depression. It is important to take care of yourself first. This is especially true if you are responsible for children or others. Put on your oxygen mask FIRST.

Your health care team's lead person could be your primary care physician. Of course, there are many specialists that may be of benefit. Psychologists, therapists, personal trainers and nutritionists are all examples of people to include in your health care team.

You may also seek alternative medicine providers such as acupuncturists, massage therapists, or energy workers to name a few. This is a personal choice and one that you can make on your own or by referrals. If this is a time of grief, try to set emotions aside as you are choosing the helpers. It is often very difficult to make decisions based on logic rather than emotions. Make sure that you know about their fee schedule, expertise and experience. Do not be fearful of asking for references. I have found that people who are very passionate about their work and the clients they serve have been my best referral partners. They often have very interesting stories about how they chose their career.

Patient Advocate

I was not aware of this resource until I became a daily money manager. My main business entailed helping people with finances. Therefore, I was not aware of many medical resources. The patient advocate often has a medical or social work background. You may also hear the term geriatric care manager. They may be independent, have a few employees, or be part of a national organization or franchise. There are pros and cons to each of these business structures. It is most important to find one that works for the individual or family rather than one that is employed by a facility. These advocates are very knowledgeable about the healthcare systems, including insurance and billing. They have usually had clients in a number of local facilities and may be familiar with staffing, food, safety and client satisfaction.

Patient advocates may accompany patients and/or family members to doctor appointments. They understand the language of medical practitioners and ask questions the family may not have thought to ask. These providers help to implement a care plan when it is warranted.

They are very familiar with health care, rehabilitation and longer-term care facilities. Most know where to find information that is not in brochures and have an understanding of how these facilities work. They may check state inspection review history as well as financial and insurance qualifications of sites being considered. They are an incredible, much-needed resource for families who are trying to care for loved ones locally or long distance.

Some may limit their practice to seniors; some may specialize in critical care. It is always wise to get several references from current or past clients when you're considering engaging a patient advocate.

Spiritual Team

Whether you have lost a loved one due to death, divorce, illness, or separation in any way, a spiritual advisor may provide great support. This person may be affiliated with a church or place of worship. They could be a pastor, minister, priest, rabbi, or other person of the clergy. This is a very personal choice and should be someone that you trust and may have known for a long while. Since there is usually no cost to visit with them or a congregation, you may certainly want to explore several before finding someone with whom you feel a connection and can fully trust.

You may also want to explore groups of like-minded people such as grief support, divorce support, etc. Again, trust your logical brain, not your emotions. With all the many wonderful, trustworthy, reputable people, there are a handful that lack strong ethics.

My father had found a great deal of support within his church after my mother passed away. He even started a Spousal Loss Group. When he was ready to explore a new relationship, he befriended a neighbor. He soon left his church and spent all his free time with his new friend. She turned out to be not such a nice person, but he had become emotionally dependent on her. She soon became financially dependent on him. He married her without the blessing of his adult children. He died several months after the marriage but not before all accounts were spent down and she was named as his beneficiary on all insurance policies.

This scenario is very common. It is heart-breaking to watch families be torn apart. You may have heard the saying, "Absence make the heart grow fonder." I have often found that money or lack thereof can also make the heart grow fonder.

Household Manager

As stated earlier, I suggest that you enlist professional help where needed. A household manager may be able to take quite a few tasks off of your plate. They may schedule maintenance, grocery shop, run errands, organize parties and do a variety of other tasks. I use this title, but someone may provide some of these services as a nanny or personal assistant. The person may be a young adult or a highly skilled organizer with an administrative background. The point is that YOU do not have to do everything. It is possible to hire others to relieve some of your duties.

A word of caution: obtain references to ensure you get reputable providers. The second important cautionary note I'll give you is to check with your tax advisor. If you are employing household help, you may be considered an employer and be required to withhold tax and report it to the IRS. Currently, this is a requirement for anyone paying wages in excess of $2200 per year. There are other criteria that should be considered to determine if they are in fact an employee or operating as an independent contractor. Your tax advisor or the IRS website may answer general questions.

Personal Advocate

A personal advocate is someone who you can truly rely upon. This may be a close friend, relative, or spouse. This person need not know all of your financial affairs. They may be the one you simply call for a shoulder to cry on. They should also make you laugh and be willing to provide honest and gentle moral support. I personally had a few of these when my husband passed.

Of course, my family was very loving and supportive but they did not live close to me. I had a girlfriend, Betty, who just knew what to do. I didn't have to ask. She was just THERE. She spent the night at my home, made phone calls, made sure we had food in the house for the first few days and kept my children entertained.

This may be a time you need support and personal connection. Hopefully you have a Betty in your life like I did. Someone who will call and insist that you join them for coffee, dinner, or a walk when you least want to interact. I found it so helpful to have people in my life who were willing to just listen or even sit in silence with me.

In addition to that emotional support, I was very fortunate to be surrounded by people who made me laugh. Those who told funny stories about my deceased husband were a welcome distraction. It's often hard to find joy in the midst of despair and grief. I also found that I felt a bit of guilt over being happy at times. Good friends will encourage and support all the different emotions without judgement.

I lost touch over time with some friends. When you are one half of a couple, socialization changes. It's not good or bad. It's just different. That aspect also requires a grieving process.

Due to the many emotions, I must again warn about emotional vulnerability. If you are offered friendship or support at a cost, walk away. The cost could be financial, emotional, or just over-dependency. The advocate I recommend should not be your only friend or relative. They should not discourage you from contact with other friends or family. If they do, this could be a red flag. Again, walk away. Sadly, I have seen this happen.

Jane was suddenly widowed. Her only daughter lived out of state. She missed the travel, dining, movies and other activities she had shared with her husband. They were close with several other couples. Jane continued to be included in the couples' dining and movie outings. She eventually stopped joining in because she felt out of place. In time, she befriended a neighbor, Max, who was charming. He was not fond of her old friends, whom he noted as her "husband's friends." He lived in the same area, drove a nice car and was always complimenting her. She found she enjoyed his company more than the single ladies she was socializing with because he paid her so much attention. He often encouraged her to change her plans with friends to join him in a different activity. Jane often offered to pay when he "forgot" *his wallet or was "waiting for a check" to come in. He moved in with her and offered to manage her investments. He always had elaborate stories of travel and boasted of a high-paying career in banking. Jane raved to her daughter how wonderful this man was and how happy he made her. It eventually came to light that he had no savings and an income that did not cover his lifestyle. As time went on, he became more reliant on Jane's money. She was not aware her accounts were dwindling until she intercepted the mail one day. Imagine her shock when she found a notice that she owed two years' worth of income tax and a statement showing her checking account overdrawn. Jane was devastated and embarrassed. She confided in an old friend, who encouraged her to leave Max. She decided to move away to be closer to her daughter but not before Max had spent over $100,000 on a new car and a boat (neither of which were in her name).*

Family

Most family members will truly want to help you. They may offer to help you with finances or introduce you to their favorite advisors. Either of these can certainly alleviate the anxiety of shopping for professionals. Questions you may pose to a family member who wants to be your investment or tax advisor include:

- What is your experience?
- How will I pay you?
- How will we have ongoing communications about my investments?

Even if a family member means well, their own choice of investments may not be the best choice for you.

Another scenario could be that a family member is expected to take over the finances. Does that person truly have the knowledge and time to step in? It may be an additional burden, particularly if they do not live close to you.

One of my current clients, Sandy, found herself depending on a remote relative. Her husband, Mike, took care of all financial matters in the household until he died. Her oldest son was then expected to take on that task. Both Mike and his son were extremely brilliant executives. Mike Jr. did step in to assist Sandy for a few months. Sandy would sometimes use a credit card or write a check from a closed account. Her son quickly realized this was more than he could handle. He had a very demanding job, a young family, and lived in another state. The family all agreed that Sandy needed someone who was not only experienced in financial matters but also patient and close enough to stop in a few times a month when needed. I was referred to the family by Sandy's financial advisor. She and her son are comforted knowing I'm there to watch over things and act as Sandy's financial advocate.

If you decide to work with a family member in any business arrangement, it is wise to have a termination discussion up front. How will you each feel if the business relationship does not work out? It is better to anticipate changes up front rather than later. It is not unusual for families to be torn apart over money. Open communication is a must in all business and monetary relationships.

Part Four:

Your Financial Legacy – Clarity, Control & Confidence

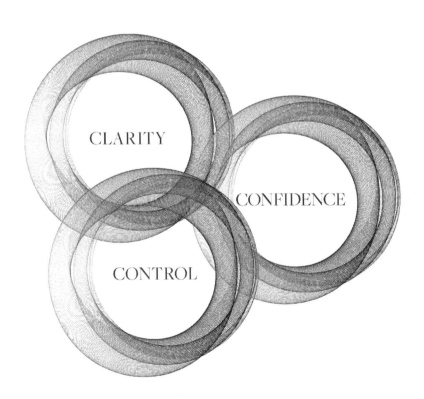

Chapter Fifteen:

Clarity

Clarity for you

I have worn eyeglasses since I was six years old. There are many times when they get smudged or foggy. I can still see (somewhat) and often put off the task of cleaning the lenses. Yet, when I do, I am always amazed at how much clearer my surroundings become. I encourage you to take the time to gain clarity of your financial life. You will be amazed by how much clearer your world becomes.

There are really only three things you can do with money: spend it, save it, or give it away. It is highly probable that the money you now have has either been earned by you or was passed on to you from someone else's hard work or savings. An exception to this could be lottery winnings or a lawsuit settlement. The beliefs and attitudes you have about money were either passed on to you or developed from experiences. How you spend, save, or give away money are lessons that you are passing to your heirs.

Clarity for others

Most people have a pretty good idea how they want their affairs and finances handled when they get sick or die. It always makes good sense to communicate your wishes. Speaking these out loud is a first step but they also need to be put in writing. We can say the same sentence to several people at different times and it is likely that our words will be interpreted in different ways. It is much easier to be specific by writing out our wishes.

Many people find communicating about wishes when facing death is very difficult. Parents don't want to upset their children or maybe they just don't want to think about it. You might say, "That is morbid. We will discuss that another time." Adult children may not want to have these conversations because they don't want to upset their parents.

Yes, it is difficult to bring up subjects such as death, illness, possessions and money. Having these conversations earlier in life before there is an event will make everyone's life easier in the long run. A good time to discuss these issues is when several family members are together at the same time. It's wise to set a convenient time for all involved. This allows everyone to prepare for the discussion.

Opening the dialogue may also be a struggle. Perhaps, someone can say, "You know my friend Sally just updated her will. When was the last time yours was updated?" Or, "My co-worker's father just passed away and his wife had no idea what he wanted. It may be wise for us to discuss your wishes." There are a number of resources to help facilitate these conversations. Both Five Wishes and The Conversation Project have online and print guides and even games to help families talk about these difficult subjects.

Chapter Sixteen

Control Plan For "What if?"

Death, divorce, illness and money are all topics that most people would rather not discuss. However, you and your family will find great peace in knowing that you have prepared for your death and helped others understand your wishes. The conversations need to be ongoing. Life changes, people change and laws change.

The best time to begin is now. If you follow the suggestions outlined in this chapter, I guarantee, you will have a new sense of freedom and empowerment.

ICE

To assist friends and family in knowing how to step in and help in an emergency, I suggest completing a document I call ICE, or "In Case of Emergency." Once completed, tell your loved ones where it will be kept. This way, you don't have to share all your personal business and account information now, but they will know where to look if you become ill or pass away. Here are items I suggest as a beginning:

Primary List

- Phone unlock code
- Voicemail password
- Email password

- Computer unlock password
- Password manager password
- Garage and house alarm code and location of spare keys
- Child and pet care directives
- Spare house and mailbox key location
- Photo copy of front and back of your wallet contents (credit cards, insurance, driver's license, loyalty cards)
- Location of legal documents such as will, trust, power of attorney

Secondary list

- Income sources and accounts receiving the income
- How bills are paid (automatic, check, credit card)
- Which accounts bills are paid from
- Where insurance policies are located (health, auto, life)
- Where to find bank, credit card, investment statements
- Safe deposit box access and contents

Additional information may be provided, but I prefer to keep this short so that it is easily compiled and updated. I suggest updating the lists at least annually. Pick a significant date so you can remember to do this, such as January 1st, your birthday, an anniversary date, etc.

I keep my list in a sealed envelope in my fire-proof safe. My safe could potentially be carried out of the house, so it's best housed somewhere that's not conspicuous. I do not keep it in my office, but instead, in the guest bedroom closet. This would not typically be the first place a thief would look should they break into my home.

Family Discussions

A well-planned family discussion is extremely valuable. Not very many people enjoy discussing their own money. General discussions about money are not difficult conversations. The price of gas, food, housing, taxes all can make for lively discussions but when it gets personal, comfort levels shift. No one enjoys having discussions about their demise. Put those two topics together and a discussion can become very uncomfortable.

It sometimes helps to mention what other friends and families have done (or not done) to bring up the topic. If you are the parent, propose that a meeting be set so that your family does not end up like Aunt Susan's, never speaking to each other again. Consider something like, "My friend Judy is so organized. She had a meeting with all of her children to let them know her wishes if she cannot speak for herself."

If you are the adult child, use the same type of conversations to open dialogue. I have found that when everyone pretty much understands the wishes of others, it is far less stressful to make decisions during a crisis. I say often because life is never perfect. People change, circumstances change, people forget and we all have emotions that ramp up during a crisis.

If you have possessions that you want a particular person to receive, write that down. This should not take the place of a will but it could make an estate settlement much smoother. You may have a rolling pin from your grandmother that you want to pass to a granddaughter who is interested in baking. Let someone know or better yet, write it down. Even though that item may not have a lot of monetary value, the recipient will appreciate the gesture and hopefully it won't get sold at an estate sale.

Preparing for the family meeting or discussion is very important. Allowing each person time to express their own fears, hopes and desires can be very productive. Here are some basic topics:

- What if financial matters become overwhelming or confusing?
- Who will take over paying bills if a parent can no longer keep up?
- Will that person be the financial power of attorney?
- Who will make medical decisions? Is that person the medical power of attorney?
- What about driving? When would a parent be comfortable giving up keys?
- Where will a parent live if unable to care for themselves or remain safe?
- What financial resources are available for housing and care?
- How will you spend your time if you are confined to your house?
- How important is social interaction?
- Would community living appeal to you?

Annual Reviews

You and your loved ones will greatly benefit from having your documents and desires updated at least annually. This task should be accomplished with a sense of love and liberation. You are providing a wonderful sense of relief for you loved ones. They will be able to focus on each other rather than digging through piles, boxes, or drawers filled with paper.

Update any changes to your health, finances, property and wishes. If one of the people you listed as a beneficiary should be removed or replaced, this is the time to do that.

Do you need to let anyone else know where your important documents are kept? Have you received any new credit cards or updated your passport? These are the items on the checklist that should be reviewed annually.

Your annual review should include your financial advisor at the very least. If appropriate, include your tax advisor, daily money manager and perhaps your estate attorney. Including them would make the most sense if there have been changes in the tax laws. If you have made any large purchases such as art or jewelry that need to be insured or your home value has increased substantially, notify your insurance agent or company.

Your financial advisor should be willing to provide you an update on your financial plan. You should be prepared to update them on your sources of income, living expenses and anticipated large purchases such as a new car or vacation. They should keep you apprised of any changes needed in your portfolio based on YOUR circumstances.

Your overall financial plan should not be driven by news of the economy or financial markets. It should be adjusted when your income changes, your expenses change, or your health changes dramatically. If you are fearful of losing money in the market, you should have an in-depth conversation about that. The worst mistake many people make is being fearful and selling investments or avoiding investing when the news is bad and markets are down. The second worst mistake is wanting to invest when the news is good. You hear of people who have made money and you want a part of that. Trying to time markets doesn't work for most people because even if they get out before a downturn, they will likely not get back in at the bottom due to fear. In reality, investing when stocks are "on sale" is the best time. Long-term successful investors stayed invested or began investing in bad markets! The best way to stay in control is to avoid acting based on emotions.

Chapter Seventeen

Confidence- You've Got This!

Putting it all together

You have taken the first step to financial confidence. You have picked up this book, opened and read some suggestions. If you implement just a few of the ideas in this book, you are ahead of most people. You have taken positive steps to improve your financial well-being.

I have had the idea for this book in my mind for years. It wasn't until COVID-19, when rest and staying inside became the norm for me, that I undertook the time-consuming and emotionally draining task of writing it. In that isolation, I was able to direct my energy into compiling this book.

My story is one of triumph, which I seldom acknowledge. I went from knowing very little about financial principles after feeling terrified about receiving a large check to dedicating my life to learning and subsequently providing guidance to others years later. My own story of helplessness to empowerment is meant to be an inspiration for you.

No matter where you are in your financial literacy journey, you can do this. Don't try to accomplish everything in a day. Just take the first step and the next ones will get easier. If you're fortunate enough to be able to plan before tragedy strikes, do it. This will save you and your loved ones headaches while in the midst of immense heartache. If you're in a place that has you devastated by grief as you struggle to understand a financial quagmire, pat yourself on the back for accomplishing the little things. Pick a manageable, important task each day and call it a big win. If you have a team, this is the time to bring them in for help.

None of this is easy but it's incredibly rewarding to feel in control. Understanding a little bit about where your money is going is a great way to start this journey. As you continue on a path of financial awareness, you'll feel more empowered than you imagined. I know. I've been there. I hope you, too, are able to dig out of wherever you're at to a place that has you feeling proud atop a money management conquest hill – or mountain. I'm cheering you on every step of the way!

I will leave you with a few of quick thoughts to consider:

- It is never too early to prepare for the future.
- Knowledge with understanding equals financial peace of mind.
- A man is not a financial plan.

A Special Gift from Teri

Now that you've read **Peace of Mind for Money Matter$**, you are on your way to moving from confused and overwhelmed to realizing clarity, control and confidence over your own finances!

As an owner of my book, I am offering a special bonus I created to add to your toolkit –**Financial Organizer Essentials.** This is a variety of tools that will help you and your loved ones gain control over financial matters that are certain to arise. The checklists, worksheets and resource links will streamline financial tasks that are often overwhelming and provide families with peace of mind.

While the **Financial Organizer Essentials** is offered for sale, as a special bonus you can claim it for free here:
http://www.day2daypersonalfinancial.com/bonus

The sooner you learn the financial basics covered in this book, the better your chances of having peace of mind over your own money matters

I'm in your corner. Let me know if I can help further.

Here's to Clarity, Control and Confidence over your financial life.

-Best,

Teri

There is no
greater wealth in this world
than peace of mind.

About the Author

Teri found her true passion later in life. She spent a quarter of a century providing financial guidance to the clients of a national firm. Determined to create a personalized service especially for women, she founded Day2day Personal Financial, LLC. Since 2017, she has been providing a customized approach designed to help her clients with their daily money management needs. She is part educator, part research pro, part taskmaster, part numbers cruncher and part cheerleader.

Originally from Suburban Detroit, Teri Rogowski had a lifetime of experiences seemingly all at once. She truly understands what it feels like to be suddenly thrust into unwanted financial transition. She was married twice, divorced and widowed at the age of 33 with four children. She had more than her fair share of heartache, stress and financial hardships. These early events provide a foundation of real-world experience which has enabled Teri to be an extraordinary educator, guide and partner to her clients.

As a single mother, she accepted a secretarial position at a financial services firm. That decision turned out to be an unexpected invitation into the world of money – and how to handle it. She studied at night to earn the licenses required to become a stockbroker which set in motion an empowering 30+ year career. Educating and empowering women in the area of personal finance became a passion.

In 1997, she was recruited to help open a branch office in Chapel Hill, North Carolina. While there, she earned the designation of Certified Financial Planner™, and Teri has provided financial guidance to hundreds of people. Her passion for helping women who are facing financial life transitions has been invaluable to many. She has hosted seminars and taught courses targeted specifically to their needs. Teri also holds the additional designation of Certified Senior Advisor, equipping her to identify the most appropriate options and solutions for the needs of seniors.

Teri serves as a dedicated partner to individuals and families seeking help and guidance to understand, organize and smoothly manage daily monetary tasks. Her oversight to personal money matters has revealed issues that are easily rectified but often overlooked. Those findings along with her experience brought about the idea to birth this book.

Connect with Teri online
Website: https://day2daypersonalfinancial.com
Facebook: https://www.facebook.com/day2daypersonalfinancial
LinkedIn: https://www.linkedin.com/in/day2daypersonalfinancial/

Made in the USA
Columbia, SC
20 May 2021